First World War
and Army of Occupation
War Diary
France, Belgium and Germany

31 DIVISION
Divisional Troops
71 Sanitary Section
1 March 1916 - 31 March 1917

WO95/2355/1

The Naval & Military Press Ltd
www.nmarchive.com
Published in association with The National Archives

Published by

The Naval & Military Press Ltd

Unit 10 Ridgewood Industrial Park,

Uckfield, East Sussex,

TN22 5QE England

Tel: +44 (0) 1825 749494

www.naval-military-press.com

www.nmarchive.com

This diary has been reprinted in facsimile from the original. Any imperfections are inevitably reproduced and the quality may fall short of modern type and cartographic standards.

© Crown Copyright
Images reproduced by permission of The National Archives, London, England, 2015.

Contents

Document type	Place/Title	Date From	Date To
Miscellaneous	WO95/2355/1 71 Sanitary Section		
Heading	31st Division Medical 71st Sanitary Section 1916 Mar-1917 Mar To 2 Army		
Heading	71st Sanitary Section Dec 16		
Heading	War Diary of from 1st March 1916 to 31st March 1916 Volume III		
War Diary	Kantara	01/03/1916	10/03/1916
War Diary	Pont Remy	11/03/1916	11/03/1916
War Diary	Hallencourt	12/03/1916	29/03/1916
War Diary	Vauchelles	30/03/1916	31/03/1916
Heading	War Diary of from 1st April 1916 to 30th April 1916 Volume IV		
War Diary	Vauchelles	01/04/1916	14/04/1916
War Diary	Bus les Artois	15/04/1916	21/04/1916
War Diary	Bus	22/04/1916	28/04/1916
War Diary	Bus Les Artois	28/04/1916	30/04/1916
Heading	War Diary of 71st Sanitary Section 21st Division from 1st May to 9th May 1916 Volume No. V Vol 3		
War Diary	Bus Les Artois	01/05/1916	31/05/1916
Heading	War Diary of 71st Sanitary Section 31st Division for 1st June to 30th June 1916 Volume No 6		
War Diary	Bus	01/06/1916	30/06/1916
Heading	War Diary of 71st Sanitary Section 31st Division From 1st July 1916 To 31st July 1916 71st Sanitary Section Volume No. 7		
War Diary	Bus	01/07/1916	06/07/1916
War Diary	Ribeaucourt	07/07/1916	08/07/1916
War Diary	Saint Venant	09/07/1916	14/07/1916
War Diary	Lestrem	15/07/1916	31/07/1916
Heading	War Diary Of 71st Sanitary Section 31st Division From 1st August To 31st August 1916 Volume 8		
War Diary	Lestrem	01/08/1916	14/08/1916
War Diary	Paradis	15/08/1916	31/08/1916
Heading	War Diary 71st Sanitary Section 31st Division September 1916		
War Diary	Paradis	01/09/1916	18/09/1916
War Diary	Locon	19/09/1916	30/09/1916
Heading	War Diary Of 71st Sanitary Section 31st Division From 1st October 1916 to 31st October 1916 Volume 10		
War Diary	Locon	01/10/1916	11/10/1916
War Diary	Terramesnil	12/10/1916	17/10/1916
War Diary	Authie	18/10/1916	31/10/1916
Heading	War Diary 71st Sanitary Section 31st Division November 1916 Volume XI		
War Diary	Authie	01/11/1916	30/11/1916
Heading	War Diary Of 71st Sanitary Section 31st Division From 1st December To 31st December 1916 Volume No. 12 Vol 10		
War Diary	Couin	01/12/1916	31/12/1916

Heading	War Diary Of 71st Sanitary Section From 1st January 1917 To 31 January 1917 Volume 13		
War Diary	Couin	01/01/1917	21/01/1917
War Diary	Bernaville	22/01/1917	31/01/1917
Heading	31st Div. 71st Sanitary Section Feb 1917		
War Diary	Bernaville	01/02/1917	20/02/1917
War Diary	Beauval	21/02/1917	28/02/1917
Heading	War Diary Of 71st Sanitary Section From 1st to 31st March 1917 Volume No. 15 Mar 1917 31st Div. Army Vol 13		
War Diary	Beauval	01/03/1917	31/03/1917

WO 95/2355/1
71 Sanitary Section

31ST DIVISION
MEDICAL

71ST SANITARY SECTION
~~MAR - DEC 1915~~
1916 MAR - 1917 MAR

To 2 ARMY

31ST DIVISION
MEDICAL

71st Sanitary Section

March 1916
April 1916

31st Div.
71 San Sect
Vol 1

Confidential

War Diary
of
71st San. Sec.

from 1st March 1916 to 31st March 1916

Volume III

March '16

Army Form C. 2118

WAR DIARY
INTELLIGENCE SUMMARY
(Erase heading not required.)

Place	Date	Hour	Summary of Events and Information	Remarks and references to Appendices
KANTARA	Mar 1		Inspection of Section 8.40 a.m. Visited A.D.M.S. (52nd incoming Division) Made final arrangements for departure of Section tomorrow. Handed over Bleam cabinet to O.C. 18th Sanitary Section (52nd Division) Obtaining receipt for same. This was urgently required in order to enable the following bacteriologically Account anid O.C. 18th Sanitary Section to the following camp areas forming out sanitary side of same; Defence Zone, Indian Mule Transport 219 Co. A.S.C., A+B incinerators, Horse Lines brother peninsular, 16th West Yorks, 271 & 223 Cos. R.E. In the evening I gave further assistance to the incoming O.C. in reference to this area. Made renewed inspection of Section.	
"	Mar 2		Section left KANTARA at mid day (with equipment, but without Motor Lorry and 2 Lorries). Arrived Port-Said 1.30 pm. Left Port-Said on "Daneervey Castle" at 9 p.m. Section (except Staff Sergt. and Sergt.) slept on deck, no other accommodation being provided.	
"	" 3		Parade of section 10 a.m and 2 pm Section put in charge of latrines and ablution places. Pte W. Green (acute rheumatism, convalescing) sent to hospital.	
"	" 4		Parade of Section 10 a.m. Off S. Taylor stopped pick Section was provided with proper sleeping accommodation Nothing requiring official report.	
	" 5		ditto	
	" 6			
	" 7			
	" 8		General inspection of Section Arrived at Marseilles at 6 a.m.	

WAR DIARY
INTELLIGENCE SUMMARY
(Erase heading not required.)

Army Form C. 2118

Place	Date	Hour	Summary of Events and Information	Remarks and references to Appendices
	Mar 9		Section left Marseilles at 11.12 pm Private Jennings reported dislocation of shoulder.	
Pont-Remy	" 10		Nothing requiring special report Section arrived at Pont-Remy at 10.30 pm. Billeted here for night except Pte Green who was transferred to Motor Ambulance at Dalon; he being to proceed with Section	Pte Green
Hallencourt	" 11		Section marched to HALLENCOURT; billets fair; called on A.D.M.S. and D.A.D.M.S	
	" 12		Parade of Section in afternoon.	
"	" 13		Inspection of Section at 9 am. Dealt summarily with charges against Pte Osborne (out of bounds at Marseilles) and Pte Green & Hayes (both absent from parade at Marseilles); 7 days C.B. and loss of 1 day's pay in each case. Subsequently these three Privates, who desired D.C.M's, saw A.D.M.S. who paid a D.C.M. on not advancing and afterwards investigated. He considered the punishment who not severe enough and forwarded me to be more severe in future. Sent M.O. Pte Benjamin & K.O.Y.L.I. and M.O. 9.2.11 + 225 R.E. in reference to Lans/cpy arrangements; attached Pte Benjamin to K.O.Y.L.I. and Pte Osgood to R.E. Pte Hayden is billeted out. Inspected sanitary arrangements of Section.	
"	" 14		Inspection of Section at 9 am; Pte Osborne said he desired to bring a charge against Staff Sergt Skinner - I told him to give the charge form in writing; he also desired to speak to Re C.J Chief against the punishment yesterday - reported same to A.D.M.S. Visited M.O. of 11th East Yorks; inspected sanitary arrangements; wrote to O.C. 3rd Aust Regarding (that it should be made compulsory for each man to have a bath twice a week and their underclothing washed once a week; Pte Osgood to advise and assist in sanitation of same	

1875 Wt. W593/826 1,000,000 4/15. J.B.C. & A. A.D.S.S./Forms/C. 2118.

WAR DIARY
INTELLIGENCE SUMMARY
(Erase heading not required.)

Army Form C. 2118

(46)

Place	Date	Hour	Summary of Events and Information	Remarks and references to Appendices
HALLENCOURT	Mar/14		Visited OC of Mobile Veterinary Section; arranged for return of prom and horse to section. Read Army Act sections 4 to 444 inclusive to Section; also paras 461 + 462 Kings Regulations	
"	15		Inspection of Section + billets at 9 am. Addressed Section in respect of their sanitary duties. Visited MO of 176th Bgde RFA; also OC of Cyclists: wrote to AA & QMG about obtaining that a water cart was urgently required for Cyclist Co.	
"	16		Inspection of (1) Section (2) Jack (3) Gas Helmets at 9 am. Visited Erondelle — no troops— 95th Field Ambulance and 165th RFA in respect of the sanitation of their units.	
"	17		Inspection of Section 9.20 am. Visited 31st Sid Supply (Sorel), 92nd Infantry Bgde Hqrs and MO 10th East Yorks, making arrangements in connection with sanitation of these units. Saw OC ASC. in respect to sanitation at his billet. Conferred with DADMS in respect of Divisional Orders 680 + 31D/26 7/3/16. Private Starks complained of & Pack and	
"	18		Inspection of Section 9.10 am: Pte Osborne of Tom's W. Officer visited him which case of scarlet fever had been removed was disinfected by Section. Visited OC Remounts; MO 11th East Lancs; 9th Field Ambulance	

Army Form C. 2118

WAR DIARY
INTELLIGENCE SUMMARY
(Erase heading not required.)

Place	Date	Hour	Summary of Events and Information	Remarks and references to Appendices
	Mar 19		O.C. Sanit. Train No 4 Coy; 13th Battalion Yorks Longs MO 169 Bgde R.F.A.; all notes elsewhere.	
	" 20		Inspection of Section 9 army. Day spent chiefly in office work. Visited Authy and Airaines (10th E.Yks & 11th E.Yks)	
	" 22		Departed on leave at short notice at 9.5 a.m. Pte Osborne to supervise sanitation of 17/St R.F.A.	
	" 28		Pte Green disinfected the whole of the billets of Lancers Hussars (remnants) by direction of D.A.D.M.S. Section left Halencourt — proceeded to Touffré	
	" 29		Section moved to Vergencourt Section moved to Beauval. Ptes Jennings (Ackroker) Smyth (Fowler) and Hayden (Cooks) left at it Casualty Clearing Station. After visiting A.D.M.S & D.A.D.M.S Sayonies	
Vauchelles	" 30		Section arrived at Vauchelles. Section in afternoon.	
	" 31		Sent two members of Section to disinfect Officers billets at Bus- Con-Artois (measles). (By request of Town Major). Section undertook charge of sanitation of Vauchelles  Dealt with complaint respecting newly erected latrines asking for particulars of alteration of 31 Division G.O.C. 31 Division C.R.E. Sanitary Section	

71 Sanitary Vol 2.

Confidential

War Diary of

from 1st April 1916 to 30th April 1916.

Volume IV

COMMITTEE FOR THE
MEDICAL HISTORY OF THE WAR
Date 9 – JUN. 1916

WAR DIARY
INTELLIGENCE SUMMARY
(Erase heading not required.)

Army Form C. 2118

(48)

Place	Date	Hour	Summary of Events and Information	Remarks and references to Appendices
Vauchelles	1 April		Inspection of Section 9.45 am. (1) Telephone Wrote to A.D.M.S. asking for allocation of units. 15th indicated 15 men. Sent Pte Osgood & Marmont to take charge Quarantine at Div Hqrs (Bus les Artois) Detailed Pte Griffiths & Taylor, J.S. to take charge of sanitation of Vauchelles. Instructed Cpl Rodd to disinfect billet from which a case of measles had been removed (Vauchelles)	
"	2 "		Inspection of Section 9.45 am: 5 men vermunous. Received location of Units from D.A.D.M.S. Instructed. by D.A.D.M.S. to visit and instruct on sanitation of Louvencourt. Detailed Pte Allan to take charge of fatigue party for sanitary duties at Bus les Artois. Pte Osgood appointed temporary Acting Lance Corporal unpaid.	
"	3 "		Inspection of Section 9.45 am. Pte Jennings (dislocation of right shoulder) and Hayden (Diarrhoea) returned to Section from 1st Canadian Clearing Station, Beauval. Called on Adjutant Divn Train A.S.C.; arranged to meet M.O. tomorrow (Louvencourt) in respect of case of measles in men billeted at Englebelmer. Visited 211 Co R.E. Billet disinfected next day. Visited Louvencourt. Found A.S.C. moving at short notice. Met M.O. of unit.	
"	4 "		Called at Bus les Artois. Inspected condition of H.Q. billets. Drew cart and paid Section to date.	
"	5 "		Inspection of Section 9.15 am. Visited Acheux in order to inspect sanitary arrangements of 12th East Yorks; unit left yesterday. Visited 10.11.12 (Transport only) & 13 East Yorks at Bertrancourt and 123/4 210 R.E. at Courcelles.	

WAR DIARY

INTELLIGENCE SUMMARY

Army Form C. 2118

(49)

Place	Date	Hour	Summary of Events and Information	Remarks and references to Appendices
Vauchelles	5 Apl	(Continued)	Detailed some of personnel of Section to supervise sanitation of the grounds	
"	6 "		Inspection of Section 9.15 am. Visited Berthencourt. Detailed 4 men of Section to supervise sanitation of this village under Town Commandant (OC 95th F.A.) Visited 15th, 16th, 17th West Yorks and D. Art (Bun le Artois) Detailed L/C Bennyman to supervise sanitary improvements required. Called on ADMS & DADMS in respect of sanitation of Divisional area. Arranged to send 3 members of Section to supervise sanitation at Bun under the Town Commandant.	
"	7 "		Spent about 2 hours inspection sanitation of Berthencourt with Town Commandant. Inspected disinfection Station at Coin. L/C Bennyman appointed full Corporal from 7/10/15.	
"	8 "		Inspected disinfector set up by 93 F.A. Vauchelles box disinfector of Section now in use by 93 F.A.	
"	9 "		Investigated & reported upon a complaint (ASC) of defective latrine accommodation. Day chiefly devoted to Office work	

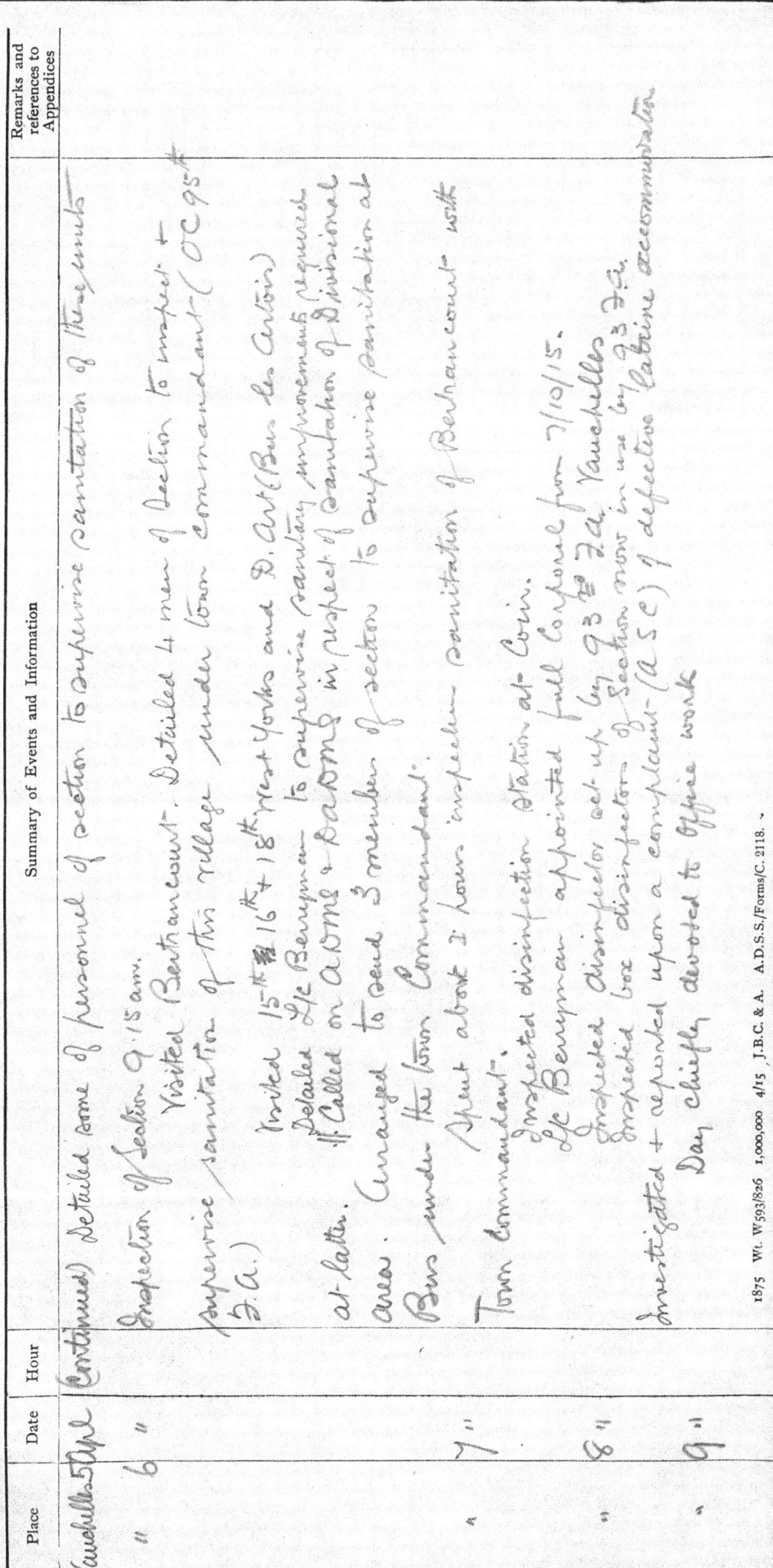

Army Form C. 2118

WAR DIARY
or
INTELLIGENCE SUMMARY
(Erase heading not required.)

Place	Date	Hour	Summary of Events and Information	Remarks and references to Appendices
Vauchelle 	April 10		Visited 165, 170, 173 Bdes RFA (Quville & Santon), saw in respect of their sanitary arrangements. Detailed Cpl. Berryman to inspect these units daily. Visited Div Ammunition Column; moving tomorrow.	
"	11		Visited Billet No 26 Vauchelles. Reported to Town Major recommending entire removal of dump hon to earth away of manure heap. Wrote to OC 165 Bde RFA in respect of insanitary condition of his area.	
"	12		Inspected pedestrian barrel set up by Sanitary Section. Visited Town Commandant at Cliencourts. Inspected baths and some of the sanitary arrangements of this area to supervise population of this area condition. Arranged for Pier Proven o Section Commandant. Saw OC 94th Field Ambulance in reference to complaint that his unit had not properly cleaned billeting area before leaving Vauchelles. Instructed by ADMS to move Section to Bus les Artois tomorrow. Occupied with other work and making arrangements connected with move.	
"	13		Section moved to Bus-les-Artois. Section took over steam disinfector which is being set up at Bus les Artois.	
"	14		Same as that of Corps. ADMS. Aperture to above.	

Army Form C. 2118

WAR DIARY
INTELLIGENCE SUMMARY
(Erase heading not required.)

Place	Date	Hour	Summary of Events and Information	Remarks and references to Appendices
Bucquoy	April 15		Saw A.D.M.S. in reference to Steam disinfector; no further progress made today. Called upon O.C. & M.O. 171 Bgde R.F.A.; arranged for L/C Fox who takes sanitary charge of SARTON, ORVILLE & AUTHIES to be attached to this unit for rations and accommodation; inspected some of the sanitary arrangements by this unit & instructions being carefully and efficiently carried out.	
"	" 16		Saw A.D.M.S. in reference to disinfecting and bathing stations; former is still ineffective; latter satisfactory being at present under the charge of this section. Called upon A.P.M. in reference to passes for the section. Called on Staff Capt. Sitzlebeh in reference to disinfecting & bathing station. Arrangements as to working and out fits of clothing made; supplied sets of underclothing drawn. Saw O.C. 94th F.A. in reference to supply of fatigue for above station. Saw Town Majors of Couincelles, Aubois & Colinisamp in reference to Sanitation of their areas. L/C Berryman & Pte Green to supervise Sanitation in the former area.	
"	April 17		Occupied in connection with disinfection & bathing station. Former commenced work about 5 p.m.; the latter incomplete. In connection with this saw A.D.M.S., A.A.& G.M.G., Town Major and the Maire.	
"	" 18		Handed over disinfecting & bathing station to 94 Field Ambulance. Withdrew personnel of section from same except Pte Osborne who remains at disinfecting station.	

Army Form C. 2118

WAR DIARY
INTELLIGENCE SUMMARY
(Erase heading not required.)

No. 52

Place	Date	Hour	Summary of Events and Information	Remarks and references to Appendices
Bus lès Artois	Mar 18		Paid Section. Inspected Gas Helmets. Section disinfected billet at which a case of German Measles had occurred. Reported existence of foul pond immediately in rear H.Q. to Town Major, Bus.	
"	" 19		Section disinfected billet occupied by case of measles at Bertrancourt. Greater part of day occupied in office work.	
"	" 20		Section disinfected to billets at Bus, in which cases of German measles had occurred. Saw M.O. 165th Bgde R.F.A. and Town Major of Sarton in respect of Sanitation; the does not report to latter offering assistance as required. Disinfected shed & tent at Bus occupied by case of German measles.	
"	" 21		Lt. Griffiths granted emergency leave for 8 days. Compiled & tabulated in pièces form part of the sanitary reports received since coming into the area. Sent to Amiens for 30 kilo Sulphur for disinfection by direction of Supply Officer A.S.C.	

Army Form C. 2118

WAR DIARY
or
INTELLIGENCE SUMMARY
(Erase heading not required.)

Place	Date	Hour	Summary of Events and Information	Remarks and references to Appendices
Bus	Apl 22		Saw Town Major Bus in reference to inspection of 91st area. Furnished ADMS with estimated amount of wood required, oil required for Dorean per week.	
"	23		Saw MO 11th East Yorks who require additional latrine buckets; referred to Town Major who has a stock. Completed tabulation of sanitary reports to date. Section disinfected billet recently occupied by case of German measles. DADMS submitted to me change Sanitary Regulation for Bus locality.	
"	24		Saw O.C. 94 F.A. in reference to Sanitary Matters. Section provided fresh lice for bathing station at Bus. Billet at Couscelles disinfected after removal of case of German measles. Inspected grease trap at bathing station. Gave instructions for using trap.	
"	25		Verbully and by letter.	
"	26		Inspected Sanitation of 165 Bgd R.F.A. Orville: saw MO of this unit; sent report to MO giving details of defects. Inspected Sanitation of D.H.Q. in company with OC him Section details for this	

WAR DIARY

INTELLIGENCE SUMMARY

Army Form C. 2118

Place	Date	Hour	Summary of Events and Information	Remarks and references to Appendices
Bus	Apl 26		Obtained from 94 F.A. list of measles cases admitted during last 10 days. 4 Bns. 1 Connells, 1 Bertrancourt; Corresponding billets have all been disinfected by section.	
"	Apl 27		Visited AUTHIES inspecting area of 165 B.A.C. 169 B.M.1 170 B.M.1 171 B.M.; sent report on sanitary condition of first, sent to M.O. Sent particulars of alleged case of measles at AUTHIES to A.D.M.S.; not reported to M.O. Billet not disinfected; contacts not isolated. Pte Osborne made acting Lance Cpl unpaid. Parade of Section at which communication 31D/5/60 G was promulgated and various orders read.	
"	28		Called upon Town Major, Authie, and Town Commandant of Septon Thievres in reference to Sanitation of their areas offering the assistance which was accepted.	

WAR DIARY or INTELLIGENCE SUMMARY

Army Form C. 2118

Place	Date	Hour	Summary of Events and Information	Remarks and references to Appendices
Bus les Artois	April 28 (cont)		Interpreter (Maurice Douineau) withdrawn from Section.	
"	29		Called upon Sanitary Officer, Santon : discussed Sanitary measures to be taken in accord with Routine Order No. 68, 4th Army (14/4/16). O/C from Section attached to Sanitary Office for inspection and supervision. Grease trap at bathing station at BUS inspected as requested by S.A.D.M.S. and report forwarded thereon. Sent No 12 KUYL in reference to Sanitation of his unit.	
"	30		Vitré Béthancourt : inspected sanitation in company with one of the men of Section allocated to this town. Two complaints of insanitary latrine (Billet 66 A.S.C. and at back of Billet 10). Both put in order in course of day ; instructed Private from Section to inspect grease trap at Bath House and see same is kept in order.	

J. O. Wakelin Barratt, Capt. R.A.M.C.
O.C. 91st Sanitary Section
31st Division

71 Sanber
Vol 3

from 1st May to 9th May 1916

COMMITTEE FOR THE
MEDICAL HISTORY OF THE WAR
Date 26 JUN. 1916

May 1916

Confidential

War Diary of [stamp: 71st SANITARY SECTION * 31st DIVISION]

Volume No V

WAR DIARY
INTELLIGENCE SUMMARY

Army Form C. 2118

(56)

Place	Date	Hour	Summary of Events and Information	Remarks and references to Appendices
Burbes Noir	May 1 1916		Inspected Billets Latrines &c at Thièvres in company with the parties in charge of this area (S.A.C.); saw M.O. and the Adjutant of D.A.C. in reference thereto; to see M.O. again in 2 days time. Visited Marieux: saw horsefall destructor (number 3B 1905) in 8 rounds of Château.	
"	2		Drew money from Field Cashier to pay section. Received two applications from civilians requesting house to cart to be sent to remove manure heaps (Nos 39 & 45 Bus.). Forwarded same to Town Major: inspected grease trap at Bathing Station, Bus; saw Sergt in Charge of Bathing Station who is anxious to work his efficiently. Section disinfected billet - case of measles at Couvelles billets of Contacts (isolation now ended) at Bernancourt. Pte Marmont ill with measles. Pte Sutton & Rogers has Ophthalmic Goitre; both removed to Canal[?] Clearing Station. Section disinfected billet & motor ambulance (German Measles);	
"	3		Visited Thièvres; saw M.O. of D.A.C.; gave him a list of major sanitary defects observed in his units area on first instant together with list of recommendations	

Army Form C. 2118

WAR DIARY
or
INTELLIGENCE SUMMARY
(Erase heading not required.)

(57)

Place	Date	Hour	Summary of Events and Information	Remarks and references to Appendices
Bois les Artois 	May 3		Inspected new incinerators for burning faeces at Marieux. Visited Sanitary Officer at Sarton; inspected incinerators (for burning faeces) in course of construction; also latrines & surface drainage. Saw N.C.O. 165th F.A. in reference to sanitary arrangements of his unit.	
"	4		Was informed that the D.A.D.M.S. proposed at an early date to send Lieut. Thompson to take over the Sanitary Section. Ascertained that a complaint made to me yesterday by the Maire respecting soiling of the ground by refuse in front of Billet No. 21 at Bus les Artois was already the subject of investigation by the Town Major with the aid of the military police. Sent member of section, by direction of A.D.M.S., to disinfect a room in No. 30 billet, in Bus les Artois, in which was a child suffering from measles. The mother of the child objected. Reported the matter to A.D.M.S. asking for further instructions.	
"	5		Occupied in writing out a report on the Sanitary Condition of the Divisional Area by request of A.D.M.S.	
"	6		Completed report and forwarded it to A.D.M.S.	

WAR DIARY
INTELLIGENCE SUMMARY
(Erase heading not required.)

Army Form C. 2118.

Place	Date	Hour	Summary of Events and Information	Remarks and references to Appendices
Bus les Artois May 6			L/Cpl Dogood granted emergency leave for 8 days.	
"	7		Section disinfected dug-out at front; also billet at Coigneux Thièvres from which a case of scarlet fever and a suspected case had been removed.	
"	8		Met Lieut. Thompson who is about to take over the section; accompanied him to the A.D.M.S. & subsequently showed him various details of my routine work and took him over to billet of the section.	
"	9		Met him. Handed section over to Lieut. Thompson by direction of A.D.M.S. introducing him to the sanitary condition of the Divisional area so far as time permitted. Received instructions from A.D.M.S. to report to D.D.M.S at Étaples.	

Army Form C. 2118

WAR DIARY
or
INTELLIGENCE SUMMARY
(Erase heading not required.)

Instructions regarding War Diaries and Intelligence Summaries are contained in F. S. Regs., Part II. and the Staff Manual respectively. Title Pages will be prepared in manuscript.

Place	Date	Hour	Summary of Events and Information	Remarks and references to Appendices
Bus-les-Artois	May 8th		Took over from Capt Barratt the 91st Sanitary Section.	
"	" 9th		Visited several outlying villages – Sarton, Authies and Thièvres. Gave orders for the numbering and testing of all wells in the Divisional Area. Had map of Couvelles traced. Gave instructions as	
"	" 10th		Inspected Couvelles and gave instructions as to type of incinerator in use at the manure dump etc.	
"	" 11th		Inspected two thirds of Bus-les-Artois.	
"	" 12th		Inspected the remaining one third of Bus-les-Artois. Arranged for latrines to be erected in different areas.	
"	" 13th		Arranged to obtain a supply of bricks.	
"	" 14th		Inspected Bucnes, Enemies and Cheenoh : also inspected work re shifting of latrine from _____. Put up a latrine for _____.	
"	" 15th		Arranged for the erection of a latrine for 15th West Yorks. Had 1000 bricks removed from SUS to Billet.	

Army Form C. 2118

WAR DIARY
or
INTELLIGENCE SUMMARY
(Erase heading not required.)

Instructions regarding War Diaries and Intelligence Summaries are contained in F.S. Regs., Part II. and the Staff Manual respectively. Title Pages will be prepared in manuscript.

Place	Date	Hour	Summary of Events and Information	Remarks and references to Appendices
Bus	May 16		Inspected Vauchelles.	
"	" 17		Inspected Bus with the object of making central permanent latrines.	
"	" 18		Inspected Couceilles. Made arrangements to start manure dump there (Couceilles)	
			Started manure dump at Bus.	
"	" 19		Inspected manure dump at Bus; also sundry sanitary erections	
"			Inspected (Colincamps) & made arrangements to start manure dump there (Colincamps).	
"	" 20		Inspected part of Orville with reference to pits for incinerators.	
"	" 21		Visited Authie and inspected sanitary arrangements	
"	" 22		Inspected Sarton, Authie & Thievres in turn.	
"	" 23 to 25			
"	" 26		Visited Colincamps and started manure dump there.	
"	" 27		Made an examination of Bus, in respect to sites for new latrines.	
"	" 28		Visited Orville. Inspected belongings to 171 Battery R.F.A.	
"	" 29		Visited Vauchelles. Made examination of water supply & general sanitation of village	
"	" 30		Visited Authie in company with D.D.M.S. and Sanitary Officer of 48th Division.	
"	" 31		Made inspection with ADMS of parts of Authie, Thievres, DAC cookhouses at Authie & the mill at Authie & pointed out defects which required remedying: viz. - of proper latrines; accumulation of filth at the horse lines, dirty cookhouses; no proper incinerators.	

signature

No. 疫 71 San
for
Vol. 4
June

COMMITTEE FOR THE
MEDICAL HISTORY OF THE WAR
5 AUG. 1915
Date

7TH SANITARY SECTION
DIVISION

War Diary of

for

1st June to 30th June 1916.

Volume No 6

Confidential

WAR DIARY

INTELLIGENCE SUMMARY

Army Form C. 2118

Place	Date	Hour	Summary of Events and Information	Remarks and references to Appendices
Bus	June 1.		Inspected Curlu's the billets occupied by DAC 31 Division along with their M.O. Pointed out that proper incinerators must be built for each unit. All latrines to be made they most that the billets themselves must be cleaned up. Gave assistance to & party of men works to build incinerator in Bar. Arranged with Town Mayor of Curlu to give him assistance to construct a tournumenter. Urged necessity for cleaning out guns etc.	
	" 2		Inspected Corbette in company with Town Major. Pointed out the condition of horse lines & told him to put D/O 1094 into force. Inspected 10th E Yorks, 11th 2.y & 13th E.Y. & Royal Irish Rifles. Wrote to the OCs regarding defects repairing latrines. Saw Capt. Baker, 93rd Bgde Machine Gun Co. gave him a written note asking him to make his latrines dust tement & for most and pointing out that ablution benches were necessary.	
	" 3		Examined billets D165 & C169 RFA. Wrote to formers and advised that no water be used for drinking purposes except after boiling; also to latter to same effect. Instructed both C.O.s to be careful as to emptying urine buckets and as to treatment of manure in accordance with Divisional Orders.	
	" 4		Sent in Sanitary Report upon weeks work to A.D.M.S. Made arrangements (unit of sanitary porter to be stationed permanently at Orville	

Instructions regarding War Diaries and Intelligence Summaries are contained in F. S. Regs., Part II. and the Staff Manual respectively. Title Pages will be prepared in manuscript.

WAR DIARY

or

~~INTELLIGENCE SUMMARY~~

(Erase heading not required.)

(4)

Army Form C. 2118

Place	Date	Hour	Summary of Events and Information	Remarks and references to Appendices
Bus	June 5		Wells (29) at Authies were tested. New fly proof latrine 6 seats finished. New brick incinerator built. No 3 incinerator Colincamps, cone erected. 11th East Yorks Colincamps, Grease Trap + covered pit made. Gave instructions to Town Major, Sauchelles to see that camp area was left tidy. Pit (4 feet cube) dug for M.Ps etc at Bus for latrine. Tent sprayed at 12th Yorks & Lancs. New incinerator started at 13 East Yorks. Arranged for new manure dump to be started at Courcelles	
"	6		Constructed:- grease trap + covered pit at Billet 35: portable fly proof cover to latrine at 12th KOYLI. Finished fly proof trench latrine at Reserve Park A.S.C: new covered urine pit at Billet 43, 10 East Yorks: grease trap + covered pit at 92nd M.G.C. Disinfected Billet No 35, Colincamps (Measles). Water Testing:- Authies, 40 wells. Inspected Harnamont Woods + arranged with new Town Major of Authies to commence new Town manure dump pointing out a probable site. Arranged for unit of Sanitary Section to be permanently stationed there to supervise the construction of latrines + incinerators required in the town.	
"	7		Constructed:- New closed urine pit at 10. E.Y Billet 26; pit + grease trap at 92 M.G.C Finished faeces incinerator at 13 E.Y: finished F.P. Trench latrine at 165 RFA. Erected F.P. boxes at Bus Wood, C170 RFA. Commenced closed incinerator D171 + C171 RFA. Finished Grease Trap + pit, Billet 54 Colincamps. Inspected spiral pump in R E lines. Water Testing - Authies - 2 wells near (a) Authies (b) Bus.	

WAR DIARY
INTELLIGENCE SUMMARY
(Erase heading not required.)

Army Form C. 2118

(5)

Place	Date	Hour	Summary of Events and Information	Remarks and references to Appendices
Bus	8 June		Constructed :- Covered pit + urine pit, Billet 26, 11 E. Yorks Colincamps. Water testing ; 26 wells at Authie. Inspected the whole of the billets evacuated by D.A.C. 31 Div. at Authie ; Gave instructions that these were to be thoroughly cleaned out and advised the Town Major re important any certificate until these were properly cleaned.	
"	9"		Constructed :- Incinerator at Colincamps ; soakage pit + grease trap + urine pit (covered) for No. 2 Sec. D.A.C. at Bus Wood. F.P. Trench Latrine. Incinerator for D171 R.F.A. Stopped the removal of a latrine at Authie and incinerator at Madeline Farm.	
"	10"		Constructed :- F.P. Cover for Latrine No. 2 Sec. D.A.C. Bus Wood; covered pit + grease trap No. 3 D.A.C. Bus Wood; new pit + grease trap for 169 R.F.A. Billet No. 10 Colincamps. Disinfected:- Billet No. 25 Colincamps. Again inspected Authie and found that Town Dennet was not being carried out properly.	
(9 ditto)			Wrote to Town Major about this and also suggested that he should apply for "permanent sweeper" now for this dist. Inspected Colincamps and visited Bullets there.	
"	11		Constructed :- New incinerator for 169 Bgd R.F.A. = Bus; Grease trap and covered pit for 11 E. Yorks, Colincamps.	

WAR DIARY
INTELLIGENCE SUMMARY

Army Form C. 2118

(6)

Place	Date	Hour	Summary of Events and Information	Remarks and references to Appendices
Bus	June 12		Constructed:- Faeces incinerator, grease trap + covered pit for D.A.C. Bus + fly proof boxes for 12th East Yorks; Bus; grease trap + covered pit for 18 West Yorks. No 6 Billet, Bus; No 5 Latrine Colincamps converted into fly proof pattern; 3 grease traps and pits for 169 Bgd R.F.A.; 1 grease trap + pit for 165 Bgd R.F.A.; officers latrine made fly proof (all at Bus).	
"	13		Constructed: new faeces incinerator; 4 urine pits, 1 soakage pit + grease trap for 169 R.F.A	
"	14		Constructed Officers F.P. Latrine for D.A.C.; atts and grease trap pit (officers cook house for 169 RFA (A B + C). D.P. Latrine (11 seats) for Couvelles.	
"	15		Constructed:- Grease trap + pit for 210 R.E.. Two urine pits for DAC N° 57 Billet. N° 9 Billet; ditto for 15th West Yorks, N° 45 Billet. Grease trap + pit for 16th West Yorks.	

WAR DIARY
INTELLIGENCE SUMMARY
(Erase heading not required.)

Army Form C. 2118.

Place	Date	Hour	Summary of Events and Information	Remarks and references to Appendices
Bus	June 16		Constructed:- 1 Latrine (sergeants) 1 Urine pit (officers) 169 R.F.A.(Bus). 1 Grease trap & covered pit 15 West Yorks, Bus. New faeces incinerator Courcelles. At Churcamps and Courcelles all cellars have been cleaned out & rubbish burnt. Arranged with Town Major, Bus. to have other incinerators erected. Wrote to Town Major, Justine pointing out the absolute necessity of obtaining fatigue parties for general work.	
"	17		Constructed:- Courcelles - New Faeces Incinerator. Bus - new faeces incinerator for 165 R.F.A.	
"	18		Inspected work at Bus and Section. H.qrs. Improved Gas Helmets of personnel.	
"	19		Constructed:- Officers latrine converted into F.P. Pattern - Bus. Faeces incinerators built for A/171 R.F.A/DAC - Bus. Urine pit (closed) for B/165 R.F.A - Bus. Grease trap & closed pit & urine pit, 15th West Yorks, Bus. Incinerator recommences at Courcelles.	

WAR DIARY
INTELLIGENCE SUMMARY

Army Form C. 2118

(8)

Place	Date	Hour	Summary of Events and Information	Remarks and references to Appendices
Bus	June 20		Constructed :- 1 Grease trap and closed pit. New faeces incinerator DAC Bus Woods.	
"	21		Constructed :- Grease trap + pit for Cyclists; billet No 79, Bus; deep trench latrine, Ordnance billet Bus. Manure dump started for R.F.A. Bus Woods. Wrote to MO DAC in reference to treatment of manure.	
"	22		Constructed :- Grease trap + covered pit for 165 RFA; four seated F.P.T. latrine behind billet Wells — fittings and fixtures repaired Bus. Latrine at ADMS office converted into F.P.	
"	23		Constructed :- 3 F.P. Trench Latrines for 171 RFA (A). 5 seat F.P. Trench latrine for 171 RFA (B). Ablution bench & soakage pit for 169 RFA (B), 1 Grease trap + pit for Hqrs 169 RFA. Wrote to Town Major stating in reference to treatment of manure.	
"	24		Constructed :- Urine pit for 165 RFA (D); 4 seat F.P.T. latrine 165 RFA (B); 7 seat F.P.T. latrine for HG RFA D.A.C. Arranged with Town Major of Couselle and Coline camps about the construction of new fly proof latrines; at Couseller an ablution bench is being removed and erected in a more suitable site. At Bus an incinerator is in course of construction. RE Signal Co in Bus have cleared out pit which was filled with rubbish.	
"	25		Constructed :- 2 F.P.T. Latrines for Billet 104, ADMS + AVC clerks offices.. 3 1 (7 seat) F.P.T. Latrine for DAC : 1 (3 seat) for C 171, RFA.. Grease trap & urine pit, Billet 9% 36, Bus.	

WAR DIARY
INTELLIGENCE SUMMARY

(Erase heading not required.)

Army Form C. 2118

Place	Date	Hour	Summary of Events and Information	Remarks and references to Appendices
Bus	June 26		Constructed (3 seats) F.P.T latrine for DAC: 1 (2 seat) F.P.T. latrine, with Officers (loose incinerator) for C171 R.F.A.	
"	27		Constructed: Grease trap and pit for billet 80. 9 Grease traps, 9 urine pits for 170, 171 & 169(D) R.F.A.	
"	28		Constructed: 10 F.P.T box latrine for 54th Field Ambulance (for Kaits)	
"	29		Constructed: 1 soakage pit & grease trap for 165 R.F.A. 4 seat F.P.T. latrine, Couicelles	
"	30		Visited Amiens, in order to settle laundry account.	

James R Thompson Lieut RAMC
OC 71 Sanitary Section

COMMITTEE FOR THE
MEDICAL HISTORY OF THE WAR
Date 31 AUG 1916

War Diary of

from 1st July 1916
to 31st July 1916

71st Sanitary Section
Volume No 7.

Confidential

Army Form C. 2118

WAR DIARY
INTELLIGENCE SUMMARY
(Erase heading not required.)

71st Sanitary Section

Place	Date	Hour	Summary of Events and Information	Remarks and references to Appendices
Bus	July 1st		Constructed: 1 J.P.T. Latrine completed (Billet No 48). Section assisted at 94th Field Ambulance. Dressing Cases. Section acted as bearers.	
"	2nd		At 94th Field Ambulance (as above)	
"	3rd		At 94th Field Ambulance (as above)	
"	4 to 6		Section engaged in sanitary work (cleaning up village) in view of early move	
RIBEAUCOURT	7		" moved to RIBEAUCOURT	
"	8		" at "	
SAINT VENANT	9		" moved to SAINT VENANT	
"	10		Units of Sanitary Section distributed over Divisional Area. Foden lorry + driver attached to Section; also despatch rider attached.	
"	11		Corpl Pratt + Pallan sent to 93rd F.A. making latrines. Harrington to 95th F.A. PUSNES St Griffiths BOFIBECQ	Ambulance Driver attached
"	12		Pte Griffiths sent to St Floris for duty with A.S.C. Units. Step taken to plant sanitary work in all areas	
"	13		Pte Bowman returned to 93rd Field Ambulance. Foden Lorry at 93rd Field Ambulance. L/Cpl Fox sent to BUS. L/Cpl Fox + Osborne returned from BUS. Both were taken over.	
"	14		Recalled men in outlying villages in view of move. Foden Lorry at 171 Bgde RFA 'C' Battery. Made preparations for departure. Billet of C.S. M case disinfected at 171 Bgd RFA D Battery	

WAR DIARY
INTELLIGENCE SUMMARY
(Erase heading not required.)

Army Form C. 2118

Instructions regarding War Diaries and Intelligence Summaries are contained in F.S. Regs., Part II. and the Staff Manual respectively. Title Pages will be prepared in manuscript.

71st Sanitary Section

Place	Date	Hour	Summary of Events and Information	Remarks and references to Appendices
Lestrem	July 15th		Section Moved to Lestrem. Started enquiries as to water supply. Obtained list of available sites for water supply for units and took steps to allot these.	
	" 16		Engaged in arranging matters concerning Baths & Laundry; also water supply. Cpl Osgood and Pte Marmont attached to 221 A.S.C. Joden lorry in use by 93rd Field Ambulance Dn'l Section. Erected an incinerator at Headquarters. Carried out unit's good water supplies to various unit's spread over to crew. Condemned some wells and advised on chlorination.	
	" 17		Baths handed over to the Section.	(102 (Peasants)
	" 18		Obtained a map of area indicating position of wells, state of supply and condition of water. Advised C.O.'s of 18th Durham L.I., 170 Bgde R.F.A. 169th Bgde R.F.A. + 210 to R.E. as to their water supply, defects in water carts and called their attention to S/o No. 904, 17/4/16. Joden lorry finished at 2 clocks (Ambulances 93+95) returned to H.Q.	
	19		Thirty five P.U. men were attached to section. Advised various units as to water supply and sanitation. Started cleansing of urine pit at D.H.Q. P.U. men were accommodated in billet, clothes disinfected and men supplied with bath.	
	20		Tabulated a list of P.U. men (Trades, Diseases etc.) and made an advance of pay to them. Appointed them to sundry work connected with the Sanitation of Divisional Area. Pte Harris sent to 93rd Field Ambulance for duty. Advised O.C. 16th West Yorks as to water supply.	

WAR DIARY
INTELLIGENCE SUMMARY
(Erase heading not required.)

Army Form C. 2118

71st Sanitary Section

Place	Date	Hour	Summary of Events and Information	Remarks and references to Appendices
Lestrem	July 21		Wrote to APM in reference to sanitation of his billet; drew attention to FS Regulation 62 para 2 & said I would give him as much assistance as possible. Incinerator started in Lestrem: also manure dumps at Lestrem RFA.	
"	22		Three dust bench latrines (F.P. seats) constructed for Section Hqs (breakwind) for L/C Griffiths. Public urinal at Lestrem reconstructed and cleaned. Units advised as to their supply, chlorination & completed water allocations. Foden lorry in use by 171 RFA "B" Battery.	
"	23		Foden lorry gunpowder by 18 West Yorks. Arranged with 171 RFA 5 and inspected the district north of Corporal Ford to be disinfected. Foden on Tuesday next. Baths:- Men bathed for week 2,705.	SM/561 P/1340. T/394. Section/393
"	24		Foden lorry allotted to 16th West Yorks; also disinfected clothing of 30 men from Hqs 171 RFA. Billet at Pont du Hem 10th East Yorks disinfected (measles case). Trench Latrines constructed for M.M.P. and one seat (hand) latrine for APM. Foden lorry allotted to 15th West Yorks	
"	25		Pte Harrington sent to 10th East Yorks for sanitary duties. Two incinerators constructed to date. Latrines (Trench) 2 F.P. Seats constructed to M. Transport (Ples Rawson & Smith reported here.	
"	26		Constructed to date (from 1st July):- F.P. Latrine Box Seats complete 29: Urinals – tin lined, Horse troughs complete 2: Ablution benches 2: Foden lorry allotted to 78th Durhams (six Engrs attached to 170 Bgde RFA (Headquarters).	
"	27		Sergt Maffin + 2 T.U. men sent to RFA 169 Bgde. 2 T.U. men sent to assist L/Cpl Osgood, 312 Divisional Train. One incinerator constructed for Battery. One Arab latrine (rail sleeper) constructed for Section. One public latrine (rail sleeper) constructed for Section.	
"	28		Foden lorry in use by 12th Yorks Lancs. A case of C.S.M. reported by ADMS: 169 Bgde RFA - billet disinfected, 4 F.P. Box seats, 1 civil ablution and one tin lined urine trough complete.	

Army Form C. 2118

(13)

1st Sanitary Section

WAR DIARY
or
INTELLIGENCE SUMMARY
(Erase heading not required.)

Place	Date	Hour	Summary of Events and Information	Remarks and references to Appendices
Lestrem	29 July		Constructed :- 4 F.P. Box Latrines : 1 Ablution bench for 14 Yorks Lavies. Corp. Lord made Acting Sergeant supercur from this date. A part of the Section, with T.V. men, were established at Vieille Chapelle for the sanitation of that district; Sergt Lord in charge. "Foden" allotted to 92nd Brigade Hqrs.	
"	30		Completed allocation of water supplies. As the water supplies are inadequate, I am endeavouring to get an extension well sunk in the Divisional area to supplement the existing supply. "Foden" allotted to 31st Divnl Train	
"	31		Constructed in the Laventie area and for units in Divisional Area, to date : 9 peace Traps, 14 F.P. Latrines, 6 incinerators (4 repaired), 4 urine pits, 2 ablution benches; 2 lin lined urine troughs complete. Foden lorry completed disinfection at 31st Divisional Train. Baths. - Clean clothing issued for week : Shirts 2805; Pants 2001; Socks 2805, Towels 2900.	

James A.R. Champney Lieut RAMC.
O.C. 1st Sanitary Section.

Confidential

War Diary of

from 1st August to 31st August 1916

August 1916

Volume 8

COMMITTEE FOR THE
MEDICAL HISTORY OF THE WAR
Date -9 OCT.1916

Army Form C. 2118

WAR DIARY
INTELLIGENCE SUMMARY
(Erase heading not required.)

Place	Date	Hour	Summary of Events and Information	Remarks and references to Appendices
Lestrem	Aug 1		Constructed: Ablution bench, floor board, for Section.	
"	2		Water: Tested 2 pumps at R.21.C.1.4 (36A): M.b. 42nd Heavy Artillery Group. Inspected Lestrem.	
			Constructed: 4 F.P. Trench latrines for 14th Yorks & Lancs.	
			Joden lorry allotted to 14th Yorks & Lancs.	
"	3		Wrote to M.O. 42nd Heavy Artillery Group (574 2/8/16) re No. Inspected Ebenezer Farm and Green Barn.	
			Constructed: 3 F.P.T. Sluices for A.V.C.: 11"PBL for 95 F.A.: 2½"PBL for Section Billets at Vielle Chapelle. 1 Complete shelter for A.V.C.	
			Joden lorry: at 14th Yorks & Lancs	
			Water: Vielle Chapelle & Richebourg St Vaast area inspected.	
"	4		Constructed: 3 F.P.T. for R.F.A. 2 F.P.B. for 31 Divisional Train at A191 R.F.A.	
			Joden lorry: Locon area inspected	
			Water:	
"	5		Constructed: Total to date F.P.T. 116: F.P.B. 53: Urinal Tops 6: Shelters 11: Incinerators 19: Ablution 5.	
			Joden lorry at B191 R.F.A.	
			Water: 92nd Brigade — Trenches inspected. Inspected Richebourg St Vaast.	

Army Form C. 2118

WAR DIARY
INTELLIGENCE SUMMARY
(Erase heading not required.)

(15)

Place	Date	Hour	Summary of Events and Information	Remarks and references to Appendices
Lestrem	Aug 6		Constructed:- 4 F.P.T. latrines for Restrem (Capt Berryman): 2 Ablution benches for Lestrem area. Foden lorry:- at 12 K.O.Y.L.I. (700 suits to be disinfected)	GRQ
"	7		Water:- Report on forward positions completed. Baths:- Clean clothing issued during week: Shirts 2968: Pants 1860: Socks 2968: Towels 2975. Constructed:- 1 Ablution bench for 31st Divisional Train. Foden lorry:- Completed at K.O.Y.L.I. Water:- Lestrem area and forward positions inspected. Inspected Bombing School and School of Instruction	GRQ Disinfection: Ambulance No 19045 - Typhoid. (95th Field Ambulance) GRQ
"	8		Constructed: 4 FPT Lat. for Officers' School of Instruction, Vacouet. 4 F.P.T. for mens Lat. Sch of Inst: 1 Urine Trough ditto 2 complete latrine shelters for School of Instruction and Bombing School. Foden lorry: 16th West Yorks Water : Lestrem and forward positions inspected — also Quentin.	GRQ
"	9		Constructed: 1 Complete latrine shelter for mens lat. Bombing School Foden lorry: 169th Bgde R.F.A. Water: Vieille Chapelle, Quentin & Lestrem areas inspected	GRQ

WAR DIARY
INTELLIGENCE SUMMARY
(Erase heading not required.)

Army Form C. 2118

Instructions regarding War Diaries and Intelligence Summaries are contained in F.S. Regs., Part II. and the Staff Manual respectively. Title Pages will be prepared in manuscript.

(16)

Place	Date	Hour	Summary of Events and Information	Remarks and references to Appendices
Lestrem	Aug 10		Constructed: 4 F.P.T at Bombing School, Pacaut. 1 Mine Trough, Bombing School	grey
"	11		Yoden Lorry; Hqrs: Blankets from 169 + 171 Bgdes R.F.A. Water: Lestrem and forward positions inspected + tested. Inspected A.S.C. at Paradis; also billet occupied by 13th East York. Richebourg St Vaast.	grey
"	12		Constructed: Inolock F.P.T. 2 B.L. 4 UT 3. Yoden Lorry: Ordnance dump and Hqrs. Water (a3) "Forward" supplies inspected + tested. (a4) Lestrem area inspected + tested. Watersupplies allotted to Units Inspected Vieille Chapelle + forwarded a list of constable places supplied to Town Major.	grey
"	13		Constructed: School of Inst. 2 F P T Complete Bat: Shelters 2. Yoden Lorry: Hqrs (trinidad workers for Ordnance Dump). Water (a5) Paradis, Pagaut, Neuville + Lestrem area inspected. (A7) Report work. Forwarded a list of wells in connection with "water" map of area to CRE.	grey
"	13		Section prepared to move to Paradis Constructed: 3 F.P.T. huts for new billet Looked for a new billet for Section.	grey
"	14		Section moved to Paradis	grey

WAR DIARY
INTELLIGENCE SUMMARY

Army Form C. 2118

Place	Date	Hour	Summary of Events and Information	Remarks and references to Appendices
Paradis	Aug 15		Section engaged in construction of Office Mess Cookhouse and latrines for mess quarters.	
"	" 16		Construction: 2 F.P.T. boxes (stock). Foden lorry: 169 R.F.A. (blankets pour tent (H9-7 for disinfection). Water: Paradis, Vacant, A&C, Vielle Chapelle & Lestrem areas inspected	grey grey
"	" 17		Construction: stock. Foden lorry: Headquarters. Water: Vielle Chapelle	grey
"	" 18		Construction: 3 F.P.T. boxes for Ordnance Dump, 18 F.P.B. boxes for Bombing School, 1 Urine Trough for Ordnance Dump, 2 Latrine shelters complete for Bombing School; 1 Ablution bench for Bombing School; 1 complete latrine shelter at Ordnance Dump. Foden lorry:- 13th East Yorks at Les Facons: 170 "A" Bgde R.F.A. blankets & tents. Water:- Domvast Area inspected	grey
"	" 19		Construction: 2 Incinerators (wet-Sutton Bastin) + Ration Dump, Fosse. Foden lorry: 13 Yorks & Lancs - "A"170 Bgde R.F.A. Water: Lestrem area inspected	grey

WAR DIARY

Army Form C. 2118

Place	Date	Hour	Summary of Events and Information	Remarks and references to Appendices
Paradis	Aug 20		Constructed : 2 Urine troughs for Vieille Chapelle Foden Lorry : Headquarters. Water : Richebourg area inspected.	Joey
"	" 21		Constructed : 2 Urine troughs for Bombing School Foden lorry : 11 East Lancs, Vieille Chapelle Water : Forward area inspected. Commenced cleaning out Moat at Adq. Chateau	Joey
"	" 22		Constructed : Stock 4 FPT boxes Foden lorry : 93rd Field Ambulance, Zelobes. Water : Loisne area inspected Inspected Reg. Aid Posts of 11th & 13th East Yorks.	Joey
"	23		Constructed : 4 F.P.T. Boxes for Vieille Chapelle : 1 Incinerator rebuilt at Vieille Chapelle Foden lorry : 93rd Field Ambulance, Zelobes Water : Headqrs water supply inspected.	Joey
"	24		Constructed : 2 FPP Latrines for Vieille Chapelle Foden lorry ; 12th York & Lancs, Lacture Water : K9 Y4 area inspected (FOSSE)	Joey

WAR DIARY
INTELLIGENCE SUMMARY
(Erase heading not required.)

Army Form C. 2118

Place	Date	Hour	Summary of Events and Information	Remarks and references to Appendices
Paradis	Aug 25		Constructed: 4 Bucket latrines FPB for Lestrem 1. Urine trough " 1 Ablution bench for School of Instruction	July
			Fodder lorry: 12 York "Kairos", Vieille Chapelle	
			Water: Merville area inspected (a.g.)	
	26		Constructed: 4 F.P.T. troop for Vieille Chapelle	July
			Fodder lorry: as above (Aug 25th) and 71 Sam. Sec.	
			Water: Vieille Chapelle area inspected	
	27		Constructed: Stock 4 F.P.T. 4 F.P.B. Hook rail for Bath. Sheds repaired with 6 sheets Corrugated iron. 2 Wale pipes for Urine Troughs. Fodder lorry: Merville for cleaning boilers. Water: Zelobes, Les Lobes, Locon, Lacouture, Le Touret inspected	July
	28		Constructed: 1 Ablution bench for Vieille Chapelle	July
			Fodder lorry: as on 27th and afterwards to 93rd Field Ambulance, Vieille Chapelle. Water: Paradis & Marmeuse inspected. Baths. Total number bathed to date (for month): Officers 121: men 9248.	

WAR DIARY
or
INTELLIGENCE SUMMARY

(Erase heading not required.)

Army Form C. 2118

(20)

Place	Date	Hour	Summary of Events and Information	Remarks and references to Appendices
Paradis	Aug 29.		Constructed: in Stock F.P.T pats 4, F.P.B. lids 4, Grease tins 1.	
			Foden Lorry: 93rd Field Ambulance	
			Water: Paradis area inspected.	
"	" 30.		Constructed: 4 F.P.T. boxes, 2 F.P.B. boxes, 1 paper case for S.A.C.	
			Foden Lorry: 93rd Field Ambulance	
			Water: Lacouture & Neuve Chapelle inspected.	
"	" 31		Constructed: 1 Urine Trough, 1 complete latrine shelter for R.A. Hqrs.	
			Foden Lorry: Neuve Chapelle — 94th Field Ambulance blankets, 93rd F.A. Kits	
			Water: Fosse area inspected. Investigated case of typhoid fever in y/317 M.B.	

James R Montre Lieut RAMC
OC 71 Sanitary Section

[Stamp: 71 SANITARY SECTION * 31st DIVISION]

140/134
V.L.g

Confidential
Oct 1916

War Diary

31st Division

71st/1 Sanitary Section

September 1916.

COMMITTEE FOR THE
MEDICAL HISTORY OF THE WAR
Date 30 OCT. 1916

Army Form C. 2118

WAR DIARY
INTELLIGENCE SUMMARY
(Erase heading not required.)

Place	Date	Hour	Summary of Events and Information	Remarks and references to Appendices
Paradis	Sep 1		Constructed: Block 5 F.P.B.: 1 Urine Trough for FOSSE area: 1 Flat paper box for FOSSE; 1 ditto for R.A. Hqrs.	Jones.
			Foden Lorry: Vieille Chapelle	
			Water:	
			Reshrew & Fosse area inspected	
"	2		Constructed: Stock 8 F.P.B : 1 Incinerator – portable for R.A Hqrs.	Jones
			Foden Lorry: Vieille Chapelle	
			Water: Rue de Paroissy to Marneuse area inspected	
"	3		Constructed: Meat safe for Section:	Jury
			Foden Lorry: Vieille Chapelle	
			Water: Merville	
"	4		Constructed: Stock 1 F.P.P. 9 sent to Vieille Chapelle. 8 F.P.B. Latrines	Jones
			Foden Lorry: 16 West Yorks, Zelobes	
			Water: La Fosse & Leshrew area inspected.	

WAR DIARY
INTELLIGENCE SUMMARY
(Erase heading not required.)

Army Form C. 2118

Place	Date	Hour	Summary of Events and Information	Remarks and references to Appendices
Paradis	Sep 5		Constructed:- Sectional work Yoden lorry; 16th West Yorks, Loleta. Water: Front, Vieille Chapelle, Croix Marmeuse area inspected	Jones
"	" 6		Constructed:- Sectional work Forties lorry; 18th Durham L.I. Y Water: Vieille Chapelle, Merville, Fosse area (also Locon) inspected.	Jones
"	" 7		Constructed:- Sectional work Yoden lorry:- Vieille Chapelle Water:- Vieille Chapelle including Baths area inspected	Jones
"	" 8		Constructed:- Sectional work Yoden lorry:- 15th West Yorks Water:- Merville, La Fosse.	Jones
"	" 9		Constructed: Sectional work Yoden lorry; Vieille Chapelle Water; Locon, La Fosse, Merville	Jones

WAR DIARY
INTELLIGENCE SUMMARY
(Erase heading not required.)

Army Form C. 2118

Place	Date	Hour	Summary of Events and Information	Remarks and references to Appendices
Paradis	Sep 10		Construction: Sectional work	
"	" 11		Jadem bom: Vieille Chapelle	
			Water: Vieille Chapelle.	
"	" 11		Construction: Smithick 13 F.P.B. Latrines; 1 Portable Incinerator; 'Ablution bench'; 3 Flat sprinklers; 3 Grease traps	Jones
			Jadem bom: 95 Field Ambulance	
			Water: Vieille Chapelle	
"	12		Construction: Beds 2 sets of 4 for Paradis; 1 Table, tin covered, for cookhouse.	Jones
			Jadem bom: 95 Field Ambulance	
			Water: Croix Barbée	
"	13		Construction: 2 F.P. Trench Latrines, Paradis. 2 Tables for messing, trestles etc complete	Jones
			Jadem bom: Field Ambulance (morning)	
			Water: Merville, Fosse.	
"	14		Construction: Cookhouse, nearly complete; 3 compartment oven, fireplace 2 boilers & sink complete.	Jones
			Jadem bom: Vieille Chapelle	
			Water: Lacture	
"	15		Construction: Sectional work	Jones
			Water: Merville	
			Jadem bom: La York Lane	

WAR DIARY
INTELLIGENCE SUMMARY
(Erase heading not required.)

Army Form C. 2118

Instructions regarding War Diaries and Intelligence Summaries are contained in F.S. Regs., Part II. and the Staff Manual respectively. Title Pages will be prepared in manuscript.

Place	Date	Hour	Summary of Events and Information	Remarks and references to Appendices
Paradis	Sep 16		Construction: Stock Iodoform, lint, Ky & E. Water: Proposed new area - preliminary inspection.	
	17		Section prepared to move to LOCON	
	18		Section engaged in moving to LOCON	
Locon	19		Constructed cook house, oven, 3 latrines; obtained particulars of water supply of new area. Constructed latrine for Dame Hugo (commenced on 17th)	
	20		Constructed 5 trench horses for Divisional Headquarters + fixed seems. Essana Baths started under Sections supervision	
	21		Water: Obtained particulars of piles + quality of water. Section engaged in cleaning new billeting area + putting same in a sanitary condition	
	22		Visited 61st Divisional Sanitary Section as directed by D.M.S. Saw workshop.	
	23		Branch Gillit at VIEILLE CHAPELLE was given up. Opened a branch at GORRE. Saw Major Rowe in reference to School of Instruction. Instructed to commence same.	
	24		Advanced position water particulars completed. School of Instruction (Sanitary) commenced.	
	25		Constructed 2 portable incinerators + F.P.B. Latrine boxes. Water - forward area inspected. Iodine Issued 95th Field Ambulance	

Army Form C. 2118.

WAR DIARY
or
INTELLIGENCE SUMMARY
(Erase heading not required.)

Instructions regarding War Diaries and Intelligence Summaries are contained in F. S. Regs., Part II. and the Staff Manual respectively. Title Pages will be prepared in manuscript.

(25)

Place	Date	Hour	Summary of Events and Information	Remarks and references to Appendices
Locon	Sep 26		Constructed — Ablution bench for Yuelle Chapelle. Jordan Lorry — Yuelle Chapelle: 9/5 Field Ambulance. Water: Forward area inspected. Jordan Lorry; Gorrenchem.	JR.Y
	27		2 Portable Incinerators built for Ration Dump A.S.C. 1 Portable (Carnation) and 1 Square (new pattern) constructed. Water: Forward area and Le Tourret district inspected. Jordan Lorry: Gorrenchem.	JR.Y
	28		Constructed: 1 Latrine for 51st D. 1 ditto (Sanitary section brand) Jordan Lorry; 0 11th East Yorks, Le Tourret. Water: Le Tourret Campion D'Action.	JR.Y
	29		Constructed: 3 Urine troughs: 1 stock: 15 bucket latrine. Jordan Lorry; 92nd Brigade Le Tourret. Water: Forward area inspected. Local sources inspected.	JR.Y
	30		Constructed for Locon Public latrines: 2 Urine troughs, 4 F.P. Boxes (bucket type) Complete shelter for same 2. Jordan Lorry; Cleaning engine boiler. Water: Locon and forward area inspected.	JR.Y

James R Unsworth
Lieut R.A.M.C.
O.C. 71 Sanitary Section

2449 Wt. W14957/M90 750,000 1/16 J.B.C. & A. Forms/C.2118/12.

140/18/1

Confidential

Oct 1916

War Diary of

from 1st October 1916 to 31st October 1916

Volume 10

COMMITTEE FOR THE
MEDICAL HISTORY OF THE WAR
Date −9 DEC. 1916

Army Form C. 2118.

71st Sanitary Section

WAR DIARY
INTELLIGENCE SUMMARY
(Erase heading not required.)

Instructions regarding War Diaries and Intelligence Summaries are contained in F. S. Regs., Part II. and the Staff Manual respectively. Title Pages will be prepared in manuscript.

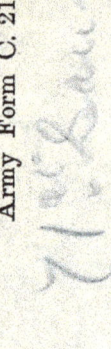

(26)

Place	Date	Hour	Summary of Events and Information	Remarks and references to Appendices
Locon.	October 1st		Constructional work for Divisional HQrs units. Water reports on forward area commenced.	
	2nd		Saw O.C. 6th Sanitary Section and gave him advice as to carrying on in this area	
	3rd		Had copies made of Water Sources reports and particulars regarding forward area	
	4th		Handed copies as above to No.4 Mobile Laboratory, Merville. Originals to be handed to O.C. 6th Sanitary Section. Sent lorry load supplies Stores to No.5 Sanitary, Marcellin, Bethune	
	5th		Completed marking water sites in the Toÿns district to-day at Bethune, 800 Blankets	
	6th		Made rehearsals for moving.	
	7th 8th			
	9th		Moving to Somme district.	
	10th		Arrived at Candas Station. Marched to Fienvillers	
	11th		Billeted at Fienvillers	
			To-day lorry sent to 95th F.A. Vauchelles. NCOs & men sent to 93, 94 & 95 F.A. for duty (sanitary). Village Cleaned. Water tested.	

Army Form C. 2118.

WAR DIARY
or
INTELLIGENCE SUMMARY
(Erase heading not required.)

Instructions regarding War Diaries and Intelligence Summaries are contained in F. S. Regs., Part II. and the Staff Manual respectively. Title Pages will be prepared in manuscript.

(27)

Place	Date	Hour	Summary of Events and Information	Remarks and references to Appendices
Tenanesnil	Oct	12	Greatest interest in village. (Sanitary arrangements very neglected). Arranged for baths to be started at Souton	
"	"	13	Started latrine in village. Water tested in Marveux, Souton, Humphries	
"	"	14	Village pitts cleaned. Water tested and various officers in various parts of Divnl Area	
"	"	15	Received report as to Sanitary condition of Souton (very bad). Sent same to A.D.M.S.	
"	"	16	Section prepared to move. Wells, notices issued affixed to wells in Tenanesnil	
"	"	17	Section engaged in moving to AUTHIE	
AUTHIE	"	18	Section established at AUTHIE. 1 NCO + 5 men sent to Couen for water duties. Took over bath at SAILY; sent 1 N.C.O. and 4 men there; also 4 men to SAILY for water duties	

2449 Wt. W14957/M90 750,000 1/16 J.B.C. & A. Forms/C.2118/12.

Army Form C. 2118.

/1st San Sec

WAR DIARY
INTELLIGENCE SUMMARY

(Erase heading not required.)

Instructions regarding War Diaries and Intelligence Summaries are contained in F. S. Regs., Part II. and the Staff Manual respectively. Title Pages will be prepared in manuscript.

Place	Date	Hour	Summary of Events and Information	Remarks and references to Appendices
Authie	Oct 19		Sent 1 N.C.O and 3 men to COUIN for Sanitary duties. SAILLY Baths started, 100 men bathed. AUTHIE village personally inspected, arranged for erection of latrines and incinerators at suitable sites. Water:- MARIEUX.	
"	20		Received particulars as to Divnl Area: following villages included :- THIEVRES, AUTHIE, COIGNEUX, ST LEGER, SAILLY, HEBUTERNE. Water:- Complete test of wells in AUTHIE récochez Notte@Bounds referred and sent. Billets. Bg. Sailly au Bois disinfected (Sulphur).	
"	21		Billet N° 65 Taken over entirely from military, Section and Laundry. Incinerator erected in Authie. Latrines constructed. Water:- Authie tested + inspected	
"	22		Inspected baths (93rd Portugese) at SAILLY au BOIS and made arrangements for improvements in same.	
"	23		Visited Amiens. Called on 18 Laundries, unable to accommodate us. Got contract for washing. Billets disinfected (XIII Corps Arra) Diphtheria. Motor Baths (40) "WALKING WOUNDED (3)" made for Ambulance.	
"	24		Made arrangements for washing clothes in villages around Septem Yemenval. Obtained names of about 30 women willing to wash clothes; also obtained a depot for distribution of civic clothing.	

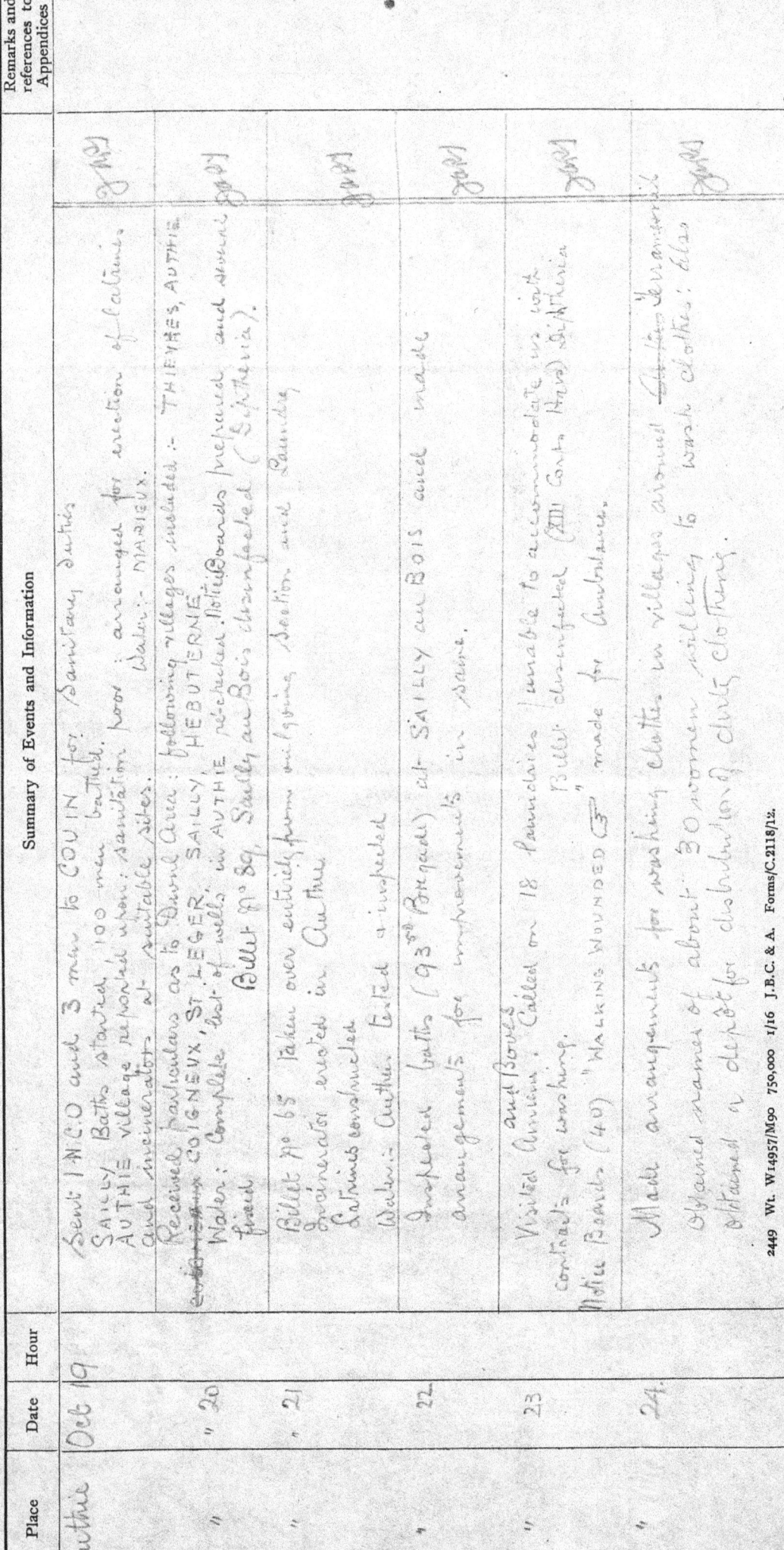

Army Form C. 2118.

WAR DIARY
INTELLIGENCE SUMMARY
(Erase heading not required.)

Place	Date	Hour	Summary of Events and Information	Remarks and references to Appendices
Authie	Oct. 25		Made further arrangements in reference to Divisional Laundry. Water laid on at Couin followed. Men returned to section. Visited Orville in reference to Laundry.	
"	Oct 26th		Reinforcement (Sgt Bentley) arrived	
"	26		50 "Walker" Warmed boxes completed for Coursellers. Couin & Sailly; Sanitation improved under supervision of latrines. Authie; 10 using pits 16 grease traps & tub washing Pits & Urinals constructed by Battalion.	
"	27		Erected a Public Urinal at Authie. Latrines at Authie & Sailly (No.2 Coy). Constructed. Visited Orville in reference to Laundry.	
"	28		Constructed: Three grease traps. 1 Latrine seat — Bucket pattern. Visited Orville & Terramesnil in reference to Laundry.	
"	29		Visited Terramesnil in reference to Laundry. Water: Couin area inspected.	
"	30		Constructed: 2 Latrine boxes, 1 grease trap. Water: Thievres, Marieux & Vauchelles, 4 Authie inspected. Visited Orville & made various arrangements for Divly Laundry.	
"	31		Constructed: 1 Grease Trap, 1 Latrine box (Bucket pattern) 1 Urine trough for Public Latrine in Authie. Water: Couin & Thievres areas inspected. Visited Baths at Sailly. The Camp at Couin.	

James E. Thompson
Lieut RAMC
OC 71 Sanitary Section

140/1862
Volume XI
Vol 9

Confidential

War Diary.

71st Sanitary Section   31st Division

November 1916.

COMMITTEE FOR THE
MEDICAL HISTORY OF THE WAR
Date -3 JAN. 1917

WAR DIARY

INTELLIGENCE SUMMARY

(Erase heading not required.)

Army Form C.2118

1st Nov letter 30

Place	Date	Hour	Summary of Events and Information	Remarks and references to Appendices
AUTHIE	Nov 1st		Constructional work: 4 Grease traps, 2 Urine troughs Water: Coigneux & Warnimont inspected Baths taken over by Baths Officer.	JR/cy
"	2nd		Constructional work: 1 Grease trap, 2 French latrine boxes Water: Coin & Coigneux areas inspected. Thiévres	JR/cy
"	3rd		Constructed: 2 Latrine seats (rails) Water: Warnimont, Coigneux, Sailly and Couin areas inspected	JR/cy
"	4th		Constructed in Section Workshops during week: 14 French boxes, 13 Grease traps, 3 Urine Troughs, 3 Soap traps, 1 Latrine complete, deep trench, fly proof, built for G.O.C. at Couin. Water: Relating and forward trenches inspected.	JR/cy
"	5		Visited Orville in reference to Laundry and payment of workpeople at Tenancesnil.	JR/cy
"	6		Arranged with O.C. 211 Co R.E. as to Latrine accommodation at new camp at Couin. Water M&t Boards affixed to supplies in Authie, Thiévres, St Leger	JR/cy

Army Form C. 2118

WAR DIARY
— or —
INTELLIGENCE SUMMARY
(Erase heading not required.)

Place	Date	Hour	Summary of Events and Information	Remarks and references to Appendices
Authie	Nov	7	Detailed report completed on water supplies and arrangements for distribution in Hébuterne and forward area. Interviewed Baths Officer re Baths Battn.	grey
		8	Constructed 2 Portable Incinerators, 4 latrine bench seats	grey
		9	Inspected Hébuterne and Sailly areas. Made arrangements with Town Majors for building public latrines.	grey
		10	Water Reports for week ending 8th sent to A.D.M.S.	grey
		11	Arranged for the building of incinerators and latrines in the Corps area.	grey
		12	Construction: 3 Grease Traps for Authie. New bench for workshop	grey
		13	Water Supplies examined: Wells bracketed; Carts labelled. Couin-Coigneux Area.	grey
		14	Constructed: 4 Trench (f.p.) latrine box seats. One incinerator (portable) corrugated iron.	grey

WAR DIARY
or
INTELLIGENCE SUMMARY

(Erase heading not required.)

Army Form C.2118

Place	Date	Hour	Summary of Events and Information	Remarks and references to Appendices
Authie	Nov 15		Commenced 1 incinerator at COIGNEUX. Constructed 8 s/p trench troughs. Water: Area inspected around COUIN	appx
"	16		Sent 5 latrine seats (trench pattern) to COUIN. Constructed 2 urine troughs. Water: Carts inspected of various units.	appx
"	17		Provided 1 portable incinerator to 221 Co A.S.C. Constructed 11 trench latrine seats in sections workshop. Water: Authie + district.	appx
"	18		Inspected Area, in company with D.M.S., of German Prisoners camp at THIEVRES. Commenced work on latrine. Gave instructions for latrine in BAYENCOURT. Water: Report of water inspection sent to A.D.M.S. Authie area inspected.	appx
"	19		Provided 2 latrines (bucket system) at German Prisoners Camp THIEVRES. 18 bucket latrine seats built + 2 shelters. Water: Coigneux district inspected.	appx
"	20		Sent 15 l/p trench latrine troughs to SAILLY BATHS for use in HEBUTERNE and arranged for erection of latrines in latter village. Water: Harrinicourt, Couin, Coigneux.	appx
"	21		Made arrangements for the erection of latrine in SAILLY village. Water - Couin, Coigneux, Sailly.	appx
"	22		Inspected BAYENCOURT. Arranged for a member of the section to undertake the supervision of sanitation of this village. Wrote to Town Major in reference to same. Water: Sailly, Thievres, Authie.	appx

Army Form C. 2118

WAR DIARY
INTELLIGENCE SUMMARY
(Erase heading not required.)

Instructions regarding War Diaries and Intelligence Summaries are contained in F. S. Regs., Part II. and the Staff Manual respectively. Title Pages will be prepared in manuscript.

Place	Date	Hour	Summary of Events and Information	Remarks and references to Appendices
Authie	Nov 23		Constructed : 10 latrine (trench boxes) : 1 ablution bench : 1 incinerator. Water : Couin, Coigneux area inspected.	July
"	Nov 24		Constructed : 3 latrine (trench) boxes for Couin : 4 (stock) : 2 urine troughs (stock)	July
"	25		Constructed : 8 Notice boards : 3 latrine (trench) boxes : 2 urine troughs & pipe. Water : Authie, Coigneux	July
"	26		Constructed : 1 Urine Trough ; completed one incinerator. Water : Couin & Bayencourt.	July
"	27		Constructed : 5 latrine boxes (trench) : one incinerator. Water : Bayencourt, Special Report.	July
"	28		Constructed : 2 latrine boxes (trench) : 2 ablution benches. Water : Couin, Coigneux area : Sailly Dell.	July
"	29		Section prepared to move to COUIN 2 Ablution benches and 1 grease trap ; also 2 pillage pits constructed for Authie village.	July
"	30		Section moved to COUIN	July

James R Thompson
Lieutenant RAMC
OC "7" Sanitation Section

2449 Wt. W14957/M90 750,000 1/16 J.B.C. & A. Forms/C.2118/12.

Confidential
Dec 1916

140/903
Vol 10

COMMITTEE FOR THE
MEDICAL HISTORY OF THE WAR
Date 31 JAN. 1917

War Diary
of

from 1st December to 31st December 1916.

Volume No 17

Army Form C. 2118.

WAR DIARY of 71st Sanitary Section

INTELLIGENCE SUMMARY

(Erase heading not required.)

(34)

Instructions regarding War Diaries and Intelligence Summaries are contained in F. S. Regs., Part II. and the Staff Manual respectively. Title Pages will be prepared in manuscript.

Place	Date	Hour	Summary of Events and Information	Remarks and references to Appendices
Couin	Dec. 1		Remainder of Section moved to Couin. Constructing corrugated iron hut to be used for Orderly Room, Store and Billet. 30'x15'.	
"	" 2		Generally improving Camp. Water; Coigneux & Sailly	
"	" 3		Further improving camp. Constructing workshop. Water; Coigneux.	
"	" 4		Improving Camp. Affixing improvised stoves to billet. Water; Coigneux & Sailly	
"	" 5		Improving workshop. Part constructing grating of fly proof for Officer N.C.O.'s + men. Water; Coigneux	
"	" 6		Fly proof latrines constructed for G.O.C. R.A. and Salvage Co. Water; Sailly & Coigneux	
"	" 7		Portable corrugated iron incinerator for R.A. Headquarters Inspected Couin and made arrangements for the erection of an also Carving and incinerator. Water; Sailly Sill	

Army Form C. 2118.

WAR DIARY of 71st Sanitary Section
~~INTELLIGENCE SUMMARY~~
(Erase heading not required.)

(35)

Instructions regarding War Diaries and Intelligence Summaries are contained in F. S. Regs., Part II. and the Staff Manual respectively. Title Pages will be prepared in manuscript.

Place	Date	Hour	Summary of Events and Information	Remarks and references to Appendices
Couin	Dec. 8		New corrugated iron chimney placed on incinerator at Couin. Water: Couin. Preparing & forwarding weekly sanitary report to A.D.M.S.	&c.
"	9		Preparing & forwarding weekly report on chlorination of water to A.D.M.S. Water: Sailly + Bayencourt.	&c.
"	10		Constructing public incinerator for Couin. Complete fly proof latrine put up for C.R.E. Water: Couigneux and Couin.	&c.
	11		Constructed:- 5 Latrine seats, 2 Urine troughs with pipes. School of Instruction: Practical work in workshops. Water: Sailly Dell & Couin.	&c.
	12		Constructed 1 Grease Trap, 1 Meat Safe, 1 Cupboard, 1 Urine pipe, 1 Soap Trap. School of Instruction: Theory & practical work. Water: Couin, Couigneux & SaillyDell.	&c.
	13		Constructed: 4 Latrine seats, 2 Urine troughs. School: Constructed 1 Incinerator, 1 Latrine seat, Grease Traps Water: Sailly. Attended Sanitary Conference	&c.
	14		Constructed: 4 Latrine seats & notice boards. School: Soap Traps & Incinerator. Water: Couin, Couigneux.	&c.
	15		Constructed: 4 Latrine seats, 1 Grease Trap & Incinerator. School:	&c.

2449 Wt. W14957/M90 750,000 1/16 J.B.C. & A. Forms/C.2118/12.

WAR DIARY of 71st Sanitary Section

INTELLIGENCE SUMMARY

(Erase heading not required.)

Army Form C. 2118.

Instructions regarding War Diaries and Intelligence Summaries are contained in F.S. Regs., Part II. and the Staff Manual respectively. Title Pages will be prepared in manuscript.

(36)

Place	Date	Hour	Summary of Events and Information	Remarks and references to Appendices
Couin	Dec 16.		Constructed: 3 Latrine seats, 1 Urine trough & pipe, 3 Traps. School: Soap traps & incinerators Water: Couin Attended Sanitary Conference	S.
"	17		Constructed: 2 Latrine seats, 1 Paper box Water: Coigneux	S.
"	18		Constructed: 1 Latrine seat, 2 Urine pipes, 1 Soap trap, 1 Paper box School: 1 Latrine seat, urine pipe, soap trap, a paper box. Water: Bailleulval	S.
"	19		Constructed: 2 Latrine seats & fittings; 2 Grease traps Water: Instructor to School. Area tested - Coigneux	S.
"	20		Constructed: 2 Latrine seats & fittings; 2 Urine troughs " (School) 1 " " 2 Soap trap, 1 Incinerator 1 grease trap Water - Couin	S.
"	21		Constructed: 1 grease trap, 1 soap trap, 1 Latrine box, 1 Paper box, 6 urine pipes, 6 notice boards. (Including School work). Water - Coigneux	S.
"	22		Constructed: 2 Latrine seats, 4 urine pipes, 3 "Old Womens Teeth", 4 Notice boards " (School) 1 incinerator 2 Latrine seats Water - Coigneux	S.

Army Form C. 2118.

WAR DIARY of 71st Sanitary Section

INTELLIGENCE SUMMARY

(Erase heading not required.)

Instructions regarding War Diaries and Intelligence Summaries are contained in F. S. Regs., Part II. and the Staff Manual respectively. Title Pages will be prepared in manuscript.

(37)

Place	Date	Hour	Summary of Events and Information	Remarks and references to Appendices
Corbie	Dec 23		Constructed:- 3 latrine seats, 1 door for cookhouse, 1 large urine trough. Second School Course ended.	&c
			Water: Coigneux	
"	24		Morning given to cleaning and improving Section cleansing area. Third School Course commenced.	&c
"	25		Christmas day	&c
"	26		School: Lectures on chlorination of water and camp sanitation. Water: 12 carts tested in Couin, Coigneux and Sailly Dell areas. Command Officer proceeded on 14 days leave Major Ware RAMC acting OC during his absence	&c
"	27		Constructed: 9 latrine seats and 2 urine troughs, nail outrights. Water: 6 carts tested in Sailly Dell district.	&c
"	28		Constructed: 1 incinerator, 2 Gear traps, 1 latrine seat - 1 urine trough, 1 complete shelter for F.P.T. latrine. Water: 6 water cart tests in Coigneux	&c
"	29		Constructed: 10 latrine seats, 2 urine troughs, 1 cookhouse sink. Water: 11 water cart tests in Coigneux	&c

Army Form C. 2118.

WAR DIARY of 91st Sanitary Section

INTELLIGENCE SUMMARY

(Erase heading not required.)

Place	Date	Hour	Summary of Events and Information	Remarks and references to Appendices
Corin	Dec 30		Constructed: 8 latrine seats, 1 urine pipe, back rails & filters. Water: Corin district. Third school course ended.	
"	" 31		Constructed 3 latrine seats, 42 filters, 2 single nails & 1 large S.P. box Water: Corin, Coignem area Fourth school course commenced.	

Geo W Ware Major RAMC
for O.C. 91 Sanitary Section

31

XI 96

14/9/1942

31st Div

War Diary of

from 1 January to 31 January
1917

Volume N° 13

[stamp: 71st SANITARY SECTION]

[stamp: COMMITTEE FOR THE MEDICAL HISTORY OF THE WAR Date 13 MAR. 1917]

Confidential

Army Form C. 2118.

WAR DIARY of 7th Sanitary Section

INTELLIGENCE SUMMARY

(Erase heading not required.)

Instructions regarding War Diaries and Intelligence Summaries are contained in F.S. Regs., Part II. and the Staff Manual respectively. Title Pages will be prepared in manuscript.

Place	Date 1917	Hour	Summary of Events and Information	Remarks and references to Appendices
COUIN	Jan 1		New trench latrine dug and camp area drained. School:- Lectures on water and practical work in workshop. Water cart tests:- 6 in COIGNEUX area	Qn.
	2		Constructed: 3 F.P.T latrine seats, 1 grease trap, 18 notice boards for water, 2 urine troughs, 1 galvanized hood for portable incinerator. School: Practical work in workshop: Lecture on Camp sanitation. Water: Cart tests, 6 in COIGNEUX area & 2 in SAILLY (DELL). Special report on COUIN water supplies	Qn.
	3		Constructed: 5 F P T latrine seats and fittings, 1 incinerator. School: Practical work in workshop + lecture on drains. Water: 9 water cart tests in COIGNEUX	Qn.
	4		Constructed: 5 latrine seats, 2 urine troughs, 1 pipe, 1 grease trap, 100 fillets, 6 notice boards. School: Lecture on water, practical work. Water: Sources of supply, inspected	Qn.
	5		Constructed: 1 latrine seat, 2 urine troughs (incinerator), 2 grease traps, 3 paper boxes, 6 notice boards (large), 12 notice boards (small). School: Practical work + lecture. Water: Special report on wells in FAMECHON.	Qn.

2449 Wt. W14957/M90 759,000 1/16 J.B.C. & A. Forms/C.2118/12.

Army Form C. 2118.

WAR DIARY
or
INTELLIGENCE SUMMARY

(Erase heading not required.)

3/7/3rd Sanitary Section 40

Place	Date	Hour	Summary of Events and Information	Remarks and references to Appendices
COUIN	Jan 6		Constructed: 2 latrine seats, 2 urine troughs, 2 large refuse boxes, 2/b refuse boxes. Completed F.D. latrine constructed at SAULTY.	
"	7		Water: 10 water cart inspections at COIGNEUX.	
"	8		Constructed: 2 latrine boxes, urine trough. Completed F.P. latrine at BAYENCOURT. Water: 14 water cart inspections at COIGNEUX and COUIN; 3 at SAULTY.	
"	9		Inspected FAMECHON. Water: COUIN area inspected.	
"	10		Constructed: Complete F.P. latrine at COUIN. Water: 11 inspections at COUIN & COIGNEUX areas; 6 in SAULTY.	
"	11		Inspected Bois Toignart. Water: Couin, Saulty areas inspected.	yes
			Constructed: 2 latrine seats. Water - Cad: inspection, Coigneux 8.	yes

Army Form C. 2118.

WAR DIARY
INTELLIGENCE SUMMARY
(Erase heading not required.)

(41)

Instructions regarding War Diaries and Intelligence Summaries are contained in F.S. Regs, Part II. and the Staff Manual respectively. Title Pages will be prepared in manuscript.

Place	Date	Hour	Summary of Events and Information	Remarks and references to Appendices
Couin	Jan 12		Tanks at BAYENCOURT inspected & report sent to A D M S. Water: Cart inspection Couprence 15, Couin 2, Bayencourt 2, Sailly Dell 8.	JA.04
	13		Reported pumping stations at HEBUTERNE - both out of working order. Water: Cart inspection: Couprence 14, Sailly Dell 8, Bayencourt 1.	JA.04
	14		Inspected BAYENCOURT & ROSSIGNOL FARM Water: Cart inspection: Sailly Dell 7, Bayencourt 1. Couprence 6.	JA.04
	15		Constructed by School. 2 latrine seats. Latrine - Chlorination of water. Water cart inspection: Couprence 10.	Inspected FAMECHON & COIGNEUX JA.04
	16		Constructed by School: 2 incinerators, 2 grease traps. Latrine: Sanitation of camps Water: Couin	Inspected SAILLY, AUTHIE & Refilling dumps JA.04
	17		Constructed by School. 1 Latrine seat, 1 grease trap, 2 soap traps. Latrine: Doctor from water. Water: Sailly	Inspected HEBUTERNE and COUIN: AUTHIE: JA.04

WAR DIARY of 71 Sanitary Section

INTELLIGENCE SUMMARY

Army Form C. 2118.

Place	Date	Hour	Summary of Events and Information	Remarks and references to Appendices
Couin	18th Jan.		Twelve of the personnel of the Section went to BERNAVILLE and 12 of 36th Sanitary Section came to COUIN.	3447
"	19th		Personnel of 36th Sanitary Sector distributed in BAYENCOURT, COUIN, ST LEGER, FAMECHON and SAILLY for Sanitary Inspection. The 12 other ranks of 71 San Sec distributed in new area BERNAVILLE	3447
	20		Prepared to move remaining half of Section	3447
	21		Handed over maps, water reports, copies of recommendations to Town Majors, and all information possible to incoming Section (No 36). Inspected TERRAMESNIL	3447
BERNAVILLE	22		Section moved to BERNAVILLE. Camp at COUIN handed over to 36 Sanitary Section	3447
	23		Engaged in putting billet in order and securing an orderly room.	3447
	24		Inspected VACQUERIE & DOMESMONT	3447
	25		Inspected LONGUEVILLETTE. Wrote to Town Majors of all villages inspected and advised as to Sanitary improvements. Prepared report for ADMS	3447
	26		Inspected HARDINVAL & HEM. Prepared water report. Wrote to Town Majors re defects in wells and water supplies.	3447
	27		Inspected PETIT OCCOCHES & LE MEILLARD Sent in weekly reports to ADMS	3447

WAR DIARY of 71st Sanitary Section (43)

Army Form C. 2118.

Place	Date	Hour	Summary of Events and Information	Remarks and references to Appendices
BERNAVILLE	Jan 28		Inspected BERNAVILLE. Wrote to Town Major re Sanitary improvements	July
"	29		Inspected GEZAINCOURT. Wrote to Town Major re Sanitary improvements	July
"	30		Inspected part of BEAUVAL	July
"	31		Attended conference at DOULLENS. Inspected remainder of BEAUVAL. Wrote to Town Major.	July

Jas R Thompson Capt RAMC
OC 71st Sanitary Section

140/1991

31st Div.

"11th Sanitary Section."

COMMITTEE FOR THE
MEDICAL HISTORY OF THE WAR
Date 4 — APR. 1917

WAR DIARY
INTELLIGENCE SUMMARY
(Erase heading not required.)

Army Form C. 2118

Vol/2

of 71st Sanitary Section (45)

Place	Date	Hour	Summary of Events and Information	Remarks and references to Appendices
BERNAVILLE	FEB 1		Inspected EPECAMPS, GRIMONT, BERNEVIL. Wrote to Town Majors re sanitation. Reported on wells to Town Majors of AUTHEUX and HARDINVAL	JRY
"	" 2		Inspected LE MEILLARD & SARTON. Reported to Town Major.	JRY
"	" 3		Inspected SARTON & AUTHEULE. Wrote to Town Majors re sanitary matters.	JRY
"	" 4		Inspected MARIEUX. Village clean but improvements in latrine accommodation required. Wrote to Town Major.	JRY
"	" 5		Inspected HEUZECOURT. Wrote to Town Major re sanitary matters.	JRY
"	" 6		Inspected BOISBERGUES. Wrote to M.O. 15West York and Town Major. " " FROHEN LEPETIT, MEZEROLLES.	JRY
"	" 7		Inspected AUTHEUX, OUTREBOIS, Mr RENALT FARM. Wrote to Town Major re accounts.	JRY
"	" 8		Inspected MARIEUX, AMPLIER. Wrote to Town Major on sundry matters. Connected with the Sanitation of their areas.	JRY
"	" 9		Inspected BERNAVILLE	JRY JRichardson Capt Sant

Army Form C. 2118.

WAR DIARY
of 71 Sanitary Section (46)
INTELLIGENCE SUMMARY
(Erase heading not required.)

Instructions regarding War Diaries and Intelligence
Summaries are contained in F. S. Regs., Part II.
and the Staff Manual respectively. Title Pages
will be prepared in manuscript.

Place	Date	Hour	Summary of Events and Information	Remarks and references to Appendices
BERNAVILLE	Feb 10		Inspected FIENVILLERS. Wrote to Town Major re sanitation of village. Forwarded weekly report to A.D.M.S. 31 Division. (in triplicate).	grey
	11		Reported to D.D.M.S. at DOULLENS at 10 a.m. (XIII Corps Hqrs). Prepared and forwarded a report shewing sanitary requirements for BEAUVAL, OUTREBOIS & GESAINCOURT areas.	grey
	12		Inspected HEM. Wrote to Town Major re sanitation of village. Visited CANDAS and saw Town Major. Village in a very insanitary condition.	grey
	13		Inspected BERNAVILLE & CANDAS. (Half the latter village.)	grey
	14		Inspected CANDAS. Completed examination of existing conditions; reported same together with fresh proposals for improvements to Town Major.	grey
	15		Inspected AMPLIER and wrote to Town Major advising him as to improvement in sanitation of this village.	grey
	16		Visited CANDAS. Wrote to Town Major, reference the dirty state of village.	grey
	17		Rendered weekly report to DDMS XIII Corps via ADMS 31 Division. Visited BEAUVAL.	grey
	18		Visited BEAUVAL with reference to move	grey

Jno R Thorpe
Capt RAMC

Army Form C. 2118.

WAR DIARY
of 71 Sanitary Section
INTELLIGENCE SUMMARY

(Erase heading not required.)

Place	Date	Hour	Summary of Events and Information	Remarks and references to Appendices
BERNAVILLE	Feb 19		NCO and 2 men took charge of supervision of BERNAVILLE area. Prepared to move remainder of Section to BEAUVAL	
"	" 20		Moving. Distribution of Section BERNAVILLE 1 NCO & 2 men, TERRAMESNIL 1 NCO & 3 men, GESANCOURT 1 NCO and 2 men, CANDAS 2 NCOS, DOULLENS 2 NCOS, BEAUVAL 1 NCO, Headquarters & NCO's & men, Water 3 men	
BEAUVAL	" 21		Completes move: Moved same to XIII Corps DDMS. Wrote to Town Major CANDAS re sites for latrines	
"	" 22		Visited MOULIENS au BOIS staging area.	
"	" 23		Received monthly reports from personnel throughout the area. Visited DDMS XIII Corps. Submitted weekly report to DDMS XIII Corps	
"	" 24		Visited TALMAS staging area. Wrote to Town Major CANDAS re protection of Personnel of the Section	
"	" 25		Inspected TALMAS area	
"	" 26		Submitted monthly report to DDMS XIII Corps	
"	" 27		Inspected MOULIENS au BOIS in morning. Visited DDMS XIII Corps in afternoon.	
"	" 28		Inspected toilets Enterprise. Inspected Well water in huts, Bernaval.	

James W. Thompson Capt. RAMC
OC 71 Sanitary Section

31

140/2043.

Vol 13

31st Div ?
4th Army

COMMITTEE FOR THE
MEDICAL HISTORY OF THE WAR
Date 11 MAY 1917

War Diary

of

[stamp: 71st SANITARY SECTION]

from 1st to 31st March 1919.

Volume N° 15

Confidential
Mar. 1919

Army Form C. 2118.

WAR DIARY
or
INTELLIGENCE SUMMARY
of 71st Sanitary Section 15/1

(Erase heading not required.)

Instructions regarding War Diaries and Intelligence Summaries are contained in F. S. Regs, Part II. and the Staff Manual respectively. Title Pages will be prepared in manuscript.

Place	Date	Hour	Summary of Events and Information	Remarks and references to Appendices
BEAUVAL	Mch 1		Inspected TALMAS, MOLLIENS au BOIS. Chose sites for sanitary requirements. Three latrines at RUBEMPRÉ disinfected.	diary
"	" 2		Inspected LA VICOGNE & PIERREGOT. Chose sites for sanitary requirements.	diary
"	" 3		Inspected HAVERNAS. Chose sites for sanitary requirements. Wrote to Town Major with reference to insanitary state of village.	diary
"	" 4		Inspected NAOURS. Wrote to Town Major with reference to insanitary conditions. Sites selected for new sanitary requirements.	diary
"	" 5		Inspected HARGNIES. Wrote to Town Major with reference to insanitary conditions.	diary
"	" 6		Inspected BERNAVILLE. Forwarded suggested Town Majors Orders to XIII Corps.	diary
"	" 7		Visited LONGUEVILLETTE: Selected new site for latrine in lieu of previous one. Trench already dug to be filled in to be in an inconvenient site for French farmers etc. Wrote T.M. re this	diary
"	" 8		Interviewed DDMS XIII Corps Doullens	diary
"	" 9		3 NCOs and one man sent to MOLLIENS AU BOIS to supervise cleaning of wells and constructing wells " " " TALMAS 1 NCO " one man "	
"	" 10		Work commenced at MOLLIENS AU BOIS. Party of 30 cyclists provided by XIII Corps. Party of 70 arrived at TALMAS for work in that area.	diary

2449 Wt. W14957/M90 750,000 1/16 J.B.C. & A. Forms/C.2118/12.

Army Form C. 2118.

WAR DIARY of 71st Sanitary Section
INTELLIGENCE SUMMARY

(Erase heading not required.)

Instructions regarding War Diaries and Intelligence Summaries are contained in F.S. Regs., Part II. and the Staff Manual respectively. Title Pages will be prepared in manuscript.

Place	Date	Hour	Summary of Events and Information	Remarks and references to Appendices
BEAUVAL	March 10th		(continued) Weekly report forwarded to D.D.M.S. XIII Corps.	gay
"	11th		Visited D.D.M.S. XIII Corps DOULLENS. Work at MOLLIENS au BOIS and TALMAS area handed over to 34th Sanitary Section. Cyclists Co withdrawn from MOLLIENS au BOIS, 3 NCOs of Section withdrawn from MOLLIENS au BOIS. Capt. Murray arrived.	gay
"	12th		Visited TALMAS area in company with Capt. Murray. Interviewed O.C. 34 Sanitary Section & handed over papers relating to TALMAS & MOLLIENS au BOIS areas.	gay
"	13th		Visited BERNAVILLE in company with Captain MURRAY	gay
"	14th		Visited GEZAINCOURT area in company with Captain MURRAY	gay
"	15th		Handed over the Command of 71st Sanitary Section to Captain T.J. MURRAY, RAMC	gay
"	16th		Visited GEZAINCOURT area: inspected various sites for new public latrines	1/n
"	17th		Interviewed D.D.M.S. XIII Corps. Submitted weekly Progress Report. Wrote to D.D.M.S. XIII Corps re Sanitary work in BEAUVAL and GEZAINCOURT. Interviewed O.C. RFC FIENVILLERS with reference to a latrine site.	1/n

2449 Wt. W14957/M90 750,000 1/16 J.B.C. & A. Forms/C.2118/12.

WAR DIARY or INTELLIGENCE SUMMARY

of 71st Sanitary Section 3

Army Form C. 2118.

(Erase heading not required.)

Place	Date	Hour	Summary of Events and Information	Remarks and references to Appendices
BEAUVAL	Mch 18th		Area of 71st Sanitary Section extended to a line drawn from COUIN to ACHEUX. Prepared to take over villages included in this area.	
"	19		Inspected BEAUVAL. Visited "Coultens" Inspected OUTREBOIS area.	
"	20th		Inspected BEAUVAL. Visited "Q" 5th Army.	
"	21st		Received instructions to take over new area	
"	22nd		Visited O.C. 10th, 36th and 62nd (Divn) Sanitary Sections and made arrangements with them to take over the following villages :- COUIN, AUTHIE, ST LEGER, FAMECHON, LOUVENCOURT, ACHEUX, ARQUEVES, LEALVILLERS, THIEVRES, VAUCHELLES.	
"	23rd		Inspected new latrines at BEAUVAL: site for manure dump. Visited Prisoners of War Camp DOULLENS road. Sent INCO and 2 men to take over LOUVENCOURT area.	
"	24th		Submitted weekly progress report to D.M.S 5th Army. Wrote to Town Major re abolition of insanitary latrine and commencement of Manure Dump.	

Army Form C. 2118.

WAR DIARY
INTELLIGENCE SUMMARY.
(Erase heading not required.)

Place	Date	Hour	Summary of Events and Information	Remarks and references to Appendices
BEAUVAL	March 25th		Sent NCO and 2 men to AUTHIE for Sanitary supervision of that area.	
"	26		Received instructions to supervise the work of 34th Sanitary Section during Capt MATTHEWS absence.	
"	27		Visited 34th Sanitary Section at TALMAS. Submitted Report for the month of March to D.M.S. 5th Army.	
"	28		Inspected BOISBERGES, OUTREBOIS, OCCOCHES. Visited CANDAS.	
"	29		Inspected water supply at MONTRELET. Interviewed Town Majors representatives with reference to same.	
"	30		Visited 21st Sanitary Section at FORCEVILLE and LEALVILLERS. Visited NCOs & men of my Section at LOUVENCOURT and AUTHIE.	
"	31		D.A.D.M.S (Sanitation) called. Inspected sanitary arrangements of BEAUVAL in company with DADMS.	
"			Called on Corps Engineer in reference to constructional work. Submitted weekly report to D M S 5th Army	

Capt. RAMC
OC 71 Sanitary Section

www.ingramcontent.com/pod-product-compliance
Lightning Source LLC
Chambersburg PA
CBHW081443160426
43193CB00013B/2366